Cardiff:
Celebration for a city

Mike Ungersma

First published in Wales in 2000 by
Hackman Printers Ltd
Cambrian Industrial Park
Clydach Vale
Tonypandy CF40 2XX
01443 441100

© 1999 Mike Ungersma

Designed by
Detheridge Limited, Cardiff

Printed and bound in South Wales
by Hackman Printers Ltd

This book may be ordered by post
direct from the publisher or design
company.

ISBN No.: 0-9537916-0-2

Contents

Foreword

It is a delight to be invited to provide a foreword to Mike Ungersma's elegant and wide ranging record of the history and contemporary scene of South Wales and Cardiff.

Latterly it describes a period during which there has been the greatest level of investment in the region since the Industrial Revolution. The regeneration of Cardiff Bay has been one important part of that and, as a consequence significantly beneficial changes in external perception and internal confidence.

The Cardiff Bay Development Corporation has been privileged to lead that process in the Bay for 12 years.

Uniquely in the United Kingdom this considerable challenge was initiated, and maintained for a significant period, with the enthusiastic support of the local authorities. This constructive political stance reflected the traditional pragmatic support of Welsh local authorities, independent of party political prejudice, to central Government initiatives.

The Corporation has worked with the local authorities, other public agencies and the private sector to provide strategic and later detailed plans for new mixed development, infrastructure and environmental improvements which has led to a dramatic increase in the confidence required for private sector investment.

Mike Ungersma's local knowledge, combined with the estimable objectivity of the professional observer, has captured sensitively the complex geographical, historical and economic components of the area.

It will provide the reader with an excellent, informed context, which I hope will encourage a visit to celebrate the reality of renaissance.

Sir Geoffrey Inkin O.B.E.
Chairman of
Cardiff Bay Development Corporation

Prologue

This is the story of a city and how its people worked to improve their community. Although such improvements are inevitably measured in terms of bricks and mortar, stones and statues, a moment's reflection reveals that this is not really what cities are about. While most of us live in cities, we tend to take them for granted, thinking only of their totality when confronted with a problem: pollution, traffic congestion, or an increase in municipal taxes. The very word 'municipality' and its Latin roots reveal more about the core meaning of a city. That Roman derivation combines the notion of a 'free city' with the idea of citizens who 'take responsibility.'

Long before there were great urban clusters of people, the ancients knew that they were a natural outcome of man's desire to be with his fellows. Aristotle, for example, called them the 'final association' of men, and noted that while they came into existence for the 'sake of life,' they soon became self-sufficient and existed for 'the good life.'

A persuasive argument could be made that for the citizens of this city, Aristotle's 'good life' is well on its way to being achieved. How one city accomplishes this and another fails raises the intriguing question of 'why?' What is clear is that in the city I write about, something happened, something took hold and gripped the imagination of thousands of people. It allowed the leaders among them to marshal the energy and enthusiasm that resulted, and direct it into a burst of civic activity that has transformed this community in a remarkably short period. And what is even more remarkable is that this happened twice in the city's recent history; first in the late 19th century and again at present.

If there is an answer to 'why?' it is very complex. We know this to be so because of those communities where the opposite happens, where in spite of the best efforts of those who would lead, the momentum is never gained, and the city remains much the same or even declines. We all know such towns and cities, places that - in the current jargon - never 'get it together.'

This is also a story that is fulsome in its praise of achievement. Great and memorable cities do not 'just happen.' They are built from the dreams and aspirations of their inhabitants. And what, after all, is wrong with dreams? As Rodgers and Hammerstein wrote in *Happytalk*, their show-stopping hit from *South Pacific*:

You gotta have a dream, you gotta have a dream,

Else how you gonna have a dream come true?

It is easy to be sceptical and even cynical about those who do have dreams, the men and women among us who have what President Bush - fumbling as always for the right words - called 'the vision thing.' The Welsh-born newscaster, Martyn Lewis, is right when he criticises fellow journalists, notorious for their cynicism, for their over-emphasis on the negative. Lewis argues: "Understanding when and why public and private efforts succeed should be as important as reporting how they fail."

But the tendency Lewis identifies extends far beyond journalism. It is what others have called the 'poverty of expectations,' a trait for which the British are widely noted that is now part of the folklore of this nation. And in Wales it is especially rife, correctly summed up in a remark attributed to former Labour leader Neil Kinnock, himself Welsh: "Nothing succeeds like success in Wales until you are." In Britain such feelings are perhaps still another remnant of relative decline. How that impacts on and is accepted by ordinary people is less well understood.

But in Wales there is, I think, another, rather more melancholy reason. These are, after all, people who have had to construct a history from the leftovers of empire, the scraps that those who ruled and commanded rejected and cast away. If there is a streak of insufficiency and even fatalism among the Welsh it is not hard to understand. Such feelings are not uncommon among people whose history includes defeat and subjugation at the hands of their neighbours or a foreign conqueror. In America, it was a century before Southerners regained the confidence they had lost as the result of defeat and occupation in a conflict many of them still refer to as not the 'Civil' war, but the 'War between the States,' and 'States' is always capitalised. Some Southern cities never recovered. Atlanta, on the other hand, even though it was razed to the ground in General Sherman's 19th century version of 'ethnic cleansing,' re-built itself into one of the most stunning and attractive cities in the world. Other cities of 'ol' Dixie' have languished. Again, one asks 'why?'

In any case, the story of Cardiff and its Bay that I tell here will not add to that already crowded genre of negativity that immensely and rightly bothers Martyn Lewis.

Americans like myself still have not lost what one might call the 'Wow!' reaction, the innocent and perhaps naive response to achievement. Like many of you, I was here during the period, the decade or so that has witnessed this second spurt of civic renewal resulting in the transfiguration of a vast area of the Welsh capital. But my 'coign of vantage,' the phrase Shakespeare used to designate that ideal place from which to witness an event, was different. I saw the story unfold through the eyes of a foreigner, and the view from another shore is always different. Perhaps, only perhaps, mine is a better understanding and appreciation of what has been accomplished.

Unlike the South, Wales did not lose a war - not a recent one anyway. But the country did suffer none the less, going through what appeared to many to be 'terminal decline.' In the name of a very short-lived period of industrial progress, Welsh valleys were laid in ruin and the best of five or more generations were yoked to a machine that cut and ground coal at one end and spat out vast quantities of riches for a handful on the other.

It is worth remembering that in Wales, not only were generations exploited in pursuit of what became known as 'black gold,' but the very earth itself was violated. Not all of the hills of Wales are the product of nature. The concentrated upheaval and destruction mining caused paid few dividends in the end. Indeed, revisionist historians may one day argue that Wales would have been much better off if the industrial revolution had begun some where else.

Thankfully, while some of the scars of that period will always remain, they have largely healed, both for the

American South and the valleys of Wales. A page in the history of both of these peoples' lives has been well and truly turned.

The reader of this account of achievement will also find no reference here to the 'good ol' days' of Tiger Bay. I invite those who wish to romanticise life in the 19th and early 20th century docks of Cardiff to look at the mortality figures for the thousands of working class occupants of the area. The Irish 'navvy' employed in the backbreaking work of the harbour - loading coal and unloading stone ballast - had a life expectancy in 1890 of around 45 years, and his wife stood an even chance of dying in childbirth.

Above all, *Cardiff* : *Celebration for a City*, is a personal chronicle of living among the Welsh in their splendid capital. The 19th century Russian intellectual, Alexander Herzen, began his memoirs with this disclaimer: "Any man is entitled to tell his story because no other man is required to listen." I can only hope you will listen.

I suppose I could say I was making a trip to the 'land of my fathers' - one of them anyway. As a boy I had always thought of myself as a Dutch-American, but not far into my childhood my father's father informed me that I was Friese, not Dutch.

First mentioned in Caesar's *Gallic Wars*, the Friese occupy the northern fringes of Holland, spill over into neighbouring Germany and on along the southern edge of the North Sea as far as Denmark. Caesar had no time for them, nor did he covet the swamps they inhabited, and marched his legions on to more important conquests. Friese names like my own frequently end in 'a' or 'ma' - Sietsma, Hockema or Wieringa or Botha. The last name, Botha, the surname of a one-time President of South Africa, is a reminder that the Friese emigrated in two directions, a tiny number going to the American Midwest and a much larger faction electing earlier for southern Africa, where they were to become the Boers and Afrikaners of more modern times. Equivalent in many ways to the American pioneers, these trekkers carved their homes from the African wilderness, becoming in their own folklore as heroic as the West's cowboys. But 200 years later their descendants made the world familiar with other Afrikaans words such as apartheid, and millions of native black Africans suffered decades of misery and injustice from the policy the word conveyed. Not that Americans behaved any better in their wilderness. As the South African ambassador to the United States was to remind me in an interview: "We settled South Africa about the same time as the Pilgrim Fathers arrived in Massachusetts. The real difference in our subsequent history is that you annihilated the native peoples. We simply wanted to live separately."

Another, more distant ancestor, my great-grandfather, was a Jones. Leaving Wales in the mid-19th century, he became a butcher in a small Midwestern town and later was to join the Northern 'Army of the Union' in the American Civil War. This kind of 'pedigree' is typical of Americans, especially those from European stock, and names like Jones, Bowen and Williams are as common in American cities as they are in Wales. Furthermore, the US mining industry owes a great deal to Welsh expertise.

Working in Europe I was to discover that the Friese and Welsh have a great deal in common. Both live on the 'fringes', geographically, politically, economically and - most of all - linguistically. And in spite of centuries of domination by their neighbours, both have somehow managed to retain much of their 'Friese-ness' and 'Welsh-ness.' For the Welsh, the preservation of their language and culture is particularly noteworthy in view of the fact that their neighbour represents the world's most powerful and pervasive tongue, English.

For the Friese that domination always came from the Dutch. Today, Frisian is the mother tongue of 54 per cent of the population of the province of Friesland, about 350,000 people. Like the English rulers of Wales, the Dutch 'allowed' the use of Frisian in education only since 1938, although it became required in primary education in 1980. Frisian is a Germanic language, closely related to English and especially Cornish. Both the English and the Dutch occasionally grumble about the concessions they are asked to make to their minorities, but surely the world is a richer and more interesting place because both of these and other minority cultures remain more or less intact.

Still another testing moment for Thomas Walker, the now forgotten engineer who built the Severn Tunnel, a marvel of Victorian technology. This contemporary drawing shows the workings flooded by an exceptionally high tide. A specialist who worked on the railways since the age of 17, Walker helped build some of the world's most difficult and challenging rail links. His career took him to Russia, Egypt, the Sudan and London, where he worked on the railway from the Thames Tunnel to Whitechapel. He built docks from Barry in South Wales to Buenos Aires.

The Severn project took virtually a quarter of his adult life, 1872 to '87. As manager of the works, he had a unique overall view of what had to be achieved. He has left a fascinating if little-read account of the experience. With the understated language he uses throughout the book, he entitled it: *The Severn Tunnel: Its Construction and Difficulties.* Toward the beginning he wrote:

> Sub-aqueous tunnels have recently become quite the fashion. One such experience as the Severn Tunnel, with its ever-varying and strangely contorted strata, and the danger of floods from above and floods from below, has been sufficient for me. One sub-aqueous tunnel is quite enough for a lifetime.

With a veritable army of more than 3,500 miners, bricklayers, plumbers, masons, carpenters and even divers, Walker tunnelled under the river and then lined it with more than 76 million bricks, most of which he made on site. It was an extraordinary achievement, ranking with today's Channel Tunnel.

In the 'Let's not embellish the facts' style he adopts throughout his book, Walker tells of the awful morning his miners were routed by a flood of Olympian proportions. Arriving at the scene of what appeared to be a disaster, he tasted the water and with relief found that it was not salty. The sea a few feet above his head had not broken in. Instead, the miners had unknowingly tapped a vast underground spring of sweet water. But it still flooded the entire works, and his force of labourers had to be evacuated. To deal with the spring, Walker built one of the most powerful steam-driven pumps ever devised and began emptying the excavation of the 24 million gallons of water that poured from the rupture each day. Astonishingly, the same pump was in use up until a few years ago. The seemingly endless spring still pours into the tunnel to this day. Every 24 hours enough fresh water is pumped from the Severn Tunnel to supply a small city.

Like the Romans nearly two millenia before him, Walker was a superb organizer of men and resources, even building his own hospital on the Welsh side of the workings to deal with the pneumonia that frequently struck down his men. The soggy, dark and dangerous conditions in which they worked are unheard of today. Walker was there on 1 July 1887, the day the first passenger train passed through his creation.

Today, tens of thousands use Walker's four-mile long tunnel each year, giving little thought to him and the men who daily risked their lives to build it. Like the engineers and designers of the first Severn traffic bridge, Walker employed pioneering techniques that were copied on countless other tunnels for decades after.

Commercially, the tunnel was as important to Wales as the M-4 motorway and the road crossings of a century later. The crossings of the Severn, above and below, have brought steady and growing prosperity to Wales and its capital. Without such links there would have been no need, no rationale for a Cardiff Bay.

Just as the Welsh rightly complain about the remnants of English chauvinism and more than imagined slights and condescension, the Friese offer similar protests about the Dutch who far outnumber them. My first encounter with this innocent insensitivity came years ago at Amsterdam's Schiphol Airport. Years before, my grandfather had warned me of their arrogance. "They boast," he declared, "that God made the Earth but the Dutch made Holland. They forget that the Friese live in the most flooded part of The Netherlands."

Following the old journalistic habit of seeking out the first barman to be encountered as a good source of information, I walked into one of the many bars that dot Schiphol. "Tell me about the Friese," I said to the man serving drinks. "Why?" he replied. "You're surely not going up there!" I replied that I was indeed since I was of Friese ancestry.

"Let's see how Friese you really are," he said, pointing to a nearby table. "Is that table round or square?"

I answered that anyone could see that it was round. "You're not Friese. Those farmers would argue until they dropped dead that it was square."

My introduction to Wales, the land writer Jan Morris called the 'damp, demanding and obsessively interesting country its own people call Cymru," was to be more benign.

A little over an hour from London's historic Paddington station, headed west on one of the world's earliest railways, the passenger senses that the train has begun to slope distinctly down hill. Here the Great Western tracks leave the flat scenery of Avon County above as they cut deeper into the earth. Suddenly the countryside disappears altogether and passengers are plunged into the darkness of the tunnel. A few fidget nervously, clearly suffering a touch of claustrophobia. Most seem pre-occupied with reading or nodding off. A minute goes by. Another two or three elapse. Clearly, a very long tunnel.

Always fascinated by technology, a habit of many Americans, I can now feel the train levelling off and then perceptibly powering up what must be a rather steep incline, grades that are usually avoided by railway builders if at all possible. As quickly as we entered the tunnel we emerge on the other side. A sign quickly flashes by welcoming us to Wales. Another says 'Severn Tunnel 1887.'

Noting my curiosity another passenger helpfully offers: "You've just come under a river, mate. The Severn River." Only later was I to see the awesome breadth of that 'river,' an expanse of unwelcome churning and swirling waters that the earliest map-makers labelled the 'Severn Sea.'

It largely goes un-remarked that Wales is bounded on the south by one of the most prominent geographical features on the planet. Even less appreciated is how it has shaped their history and thinking. A legacy of the Ice Age, the 'bite' the Atlantic Ocean takes out of Britain's western shore is the most notable characteristic of a map of the country, and must have been recognised immediately by the first British astronaut. Only occasionally are the Welsh reminded of the 'sea' that forms their only geographic border with their English neighbour. While argument may rage about the boundary to the east, the famous 'Marches,' and just where Wales historically began and England

As workers delicately lower a section of the second Severn crossing into place, Teranda negotiates the 'Severn Sea,' one of the most awkward estuaries in the world for sailors. Twice each day the world's second highest tides push in from the open Atlantic against the Severn's already powerful currents, a vast water drainage system that is fed from rivers and streams in both England and Wales. As the two meet, smaller ships and especially yachts and cruisers like Teranda are guaranteed a very rough ride, even in the best of weather. And when 'so'westers' blow across an outgoing tide reinforced by the current, conditions can become precarious on a coast where there are few safe places to shelter. In the past, sailing ships would run to the relative safety of the Taff and Ely Rivers even though an outgoing tide meant they would were almost certain to be left stranded for hours or even days on Cardiff Bay's mud flats. Soon pleasure boats will be able to take refuge behind the sea wall in front the new barrage at any state of the tide.

than either an emperor or a king could ever hope to construct. Like the 'English' Channel separating the United Kingdom from Europe, the unvanquished English have the privilege of calling it whatever they wish. It is also indisputable that this is one of the most treacherous stretches of water on our globe, what one sailor described as a 'bubbling malevolence.' Today, visitors to Cardiff pass over it, above it or under it. But for most of Wales' history, moving along the settlements that dotted the southern coast of the country, or the historic English bank of Avon, Somerset and Devon, was done by sea. Only tourists on summer pleasure boats such as the historic Waverley, and its sister ship, Balmoral, can get a flavour of what using the Severn actually meant in an era when men had to go to sea.

But what is even more curious is that this experience, this proximity to the sea never produced a great Welsh maritime figure, culture or even industry. With a country whose borders are mostly coastline, a country that can boast of a great natural harbour like Milford Haven, why are there no Magellans, Cooks, Nelsons or Vasco de Gamas? Why did the sea not become the highway for the Welsh that it became for other peoples? Why is it that the only great historic ports of the Irish Sea are Liverpool and Gloucester and Bristol - all in England? Cardiff, Barry and Newport rose and then declined in a very short period, and almost entirely due to coal. While only few ports outside London and a handful along the English Channel remain viable and active, none in Wales has enjoyed anything but fleeting and temporary fame.

Dun Sands, English Stones, Denny Shoal and Welsh Hook, names I would soon know intimately. All are from nautical charts, the highly detailed maps of the seas that are to a sailor what the 'Road Atlas' is to the ended, there can be no quibble about this border: what you see across the mighty Severn to the south was once a foreign shore.

Tourists who visit Britain marvel at Hadrian's Wall, the snaking 73 mile long fortification built by the Emperor Hadrian as a defence against 'barbarian' invasions of his Roman colony from the north. Constructed in the remarkably short space of four years, it completely spans the narrow neck of northern England from Newcastle in the east to Drumburgh in the west. Historians regard it as the most impressive of all Roman frontier works anywhere in their vast empire.

Wales has a similar, but far less known frontier fortification: Offa's Dyke. Built by the King of Mercia in 785 AD, more than six centuries after Hadrian completed his formidable wall, it is an earthwork structure, and nearly twice as long as the Roman wall of mostly stone. From the estuary of the River Dee in North Wales to the River Severn in the south of the country, the Dyke was an exceptional engineering achievement for its time, and took advantage of the natural features of the land. King Offa ruled over a medieval Anglo-Saxon kingdom bordered on the west by the hostile Welsh, and like the Romans before him, had little interest in their country apart from subduing them. The dyke was intended to keep them in their remote corner of the British Isles, and today pretty much marks the modern border between England and Wales. In more recent history, the line between the two nations was often fought over countless times, with the English invaders almost invariably and ultimately triumphant. But there is no disputing the southern boundary of Wales, variously the 'Severn Estuary' or the 'Bristol Channel,' a divide mightier

'Hafren,' Welsh for Severn, reveals the river's fickle nature. Not only does it spectacularly separate Wales from England's 'West Country' to the south, but its first half teases its way in and out of the Principality like a woman may in a man's heart. The word means 'trollop.'

Here, 'Pont Hafren' became the first road bridge across the mighty river. It opened to traffic in 1969 with a blessing from the Queen and replaced a ferry that had operated since medieval times, a fact revealed only recently by the discovery of ancient records kept by the monks of the picturesque and nearby Tintern Abbey, made famous by the poetry of Wordsworth.

Like Walker's tunnel, the bridge became a model of innovative construction and its design was repeated virtually unchanged over another treacherous body of water, the Straits of Bosporus in Turkey where Europe is said to end and Asia begin.

motorist. I had been under, over and even above the Severn. Now I had to chance to sail on it, and would do so for almost its entire navigable length. Several summers ago a friend bought a cruiser in Upton-on-Severn and asked me to bring it down the River and into the estuary, ultimately to that unique place of solace and refuge for so many ships and sailors, Milford Haven.

Britain's longest river, the Severn begins in Wales, winds its way placidly through the hills of the middle part of the country, and then into England. Up until 150 years ago, goods carried by boat could reach as far as Poll Quay in Welshpool, well above Upton where my journey was to begin. Now only pleasure boats can make that trip, and then only a few miles upriver from Upton. This is the heart of Gloucestershire, the pleasant English county known to Americans for the Cotswolds and the home of composer Edward Elgar.

Quiet and meandering for roughly half its path to the sea, the Severn could be said to suffer from a severe case of 'split personality.' It is at Gloucester itself that its darker and more sinister side begins to emerge. Here, as Tennyson wrote,

There twice a day the Severn fills;

The salt sea-water passes by,

And hushes half the babbling Wye,

And makes a silence in the hills.

For here the river turns its face west. Here also it broadens and widens to Mississippi proportions. And here also it becomes tidal, very tidal. As any Welshman will tell you, the Severn has the second highest tidal range in the world, an obscure Canadian river in the Bay of Fundy claiming title to the first. Forget about the tides of France's Mont Saint Michel, as impressive and even frightening as they can be. Here is an estuary facing the total force of an ocean. For more than one hundred miles it widens into a giant funnel, and twice each day accepts the tides of an Atlantic unhindered by any other trace of land before the Americas. For the sailor, this is where the ocean really begins, not at Cardiff, Swansea or even Milford Haven and its 'Western Approaches,' familiar to American naval ships of World War II.

The charts produced by the British Admiralty reveal the real nature of the river once it leaves Gloucester. With typical British understatement, one note to mariners reads: "Above King Road navigation is not advisable without local knowledge." Near the still-busy commercial harbour of Avonmouth, the port nearest Bristol, another warning quietly admonishes: "Here tidal streams run from 3 to 8 knots and there is little slack water." Sir Francis Chichester would have thought twice about negotiating such challenges 'without local knowledge.' As it turned out, neither would I.

From Upton to Gloucester is the 'weekend sailor's' dream. Although it remains a shipping channel, the only 'shipping' is cargoes of grain carried as they have been for centuries, on barges that still ply the Severn from Gloucester to the mill at Tewkesbury. Proving the saying that 'All travel is time travel,' the river here is a living instead of a written history.

A month of reconnaissance began before I was ready to 'drop the moorings' at Upton's pleasant marina and begin the trip to the sea. I studied this river by walking and driving to countless locations along its shores, English and Welsh. I was to learn a great deal about it and the people on both banks. One of many discoveries was the two yacht clubs that actually use this tidal reach of the Severn for fun. I could understand the literally hundreds of recreational boats that make the upper, non-tidal Severn their base, but not this section. The area includes a 25 mile long stretch of the Severn that has never been navigable. Indeed, it is so hostile that a canal was built alongside the river to accommodate sea-bound commercial traffic from Gloucester. The canal terminates at Sharpness with huge locks that can accept ocean-going vessels, and still does.

This is also the part of the river that produces the famous 'Severn bore,' a phenomenon rare to rivers anywhere. Such is the force of the tide, especially the monthly 'spring' tides, that when combined with especially strong and frequent westerly gales, it produces a tidal wave or 'bore' that can be six feet high and travel upriver towards Gloucester at ten miles an hour. It can be and is surfed by the daring.

So famous is the bore that one enthusiast, Robin Harvey, has set up a site on the Internet giving the curious the best times and locations to see one of the natural wonders of this remarkable river. But Robin also dryly warns that "Following the initial bore wave, there is a substantial rise in water level for an hour or so. Please take care where you stand or park as a number of spectators or cars had to be rescued by the Police in recent years."

The thousands who have seen the bore are rarely disappointed. Even at night it can be frighteningly impressive. They speak of the 'muffled thunder-like sound' as it approaches, and a brown wave that sweeps past in seconds, bending saplings double on both banks.

The canal to Sharpness avoids this section where no boat dare go, and it is at this point that only serious and experienced sailors, commercial or pleasure, venture forth. A tiny community supports this working harbour where cargoes of mostly scrap metal are loaded for export and wood from abroad is received. The Teranda, the 36 foot cruiser I was taking down-river, called there and spent a night while I searched for someone with 'local knowledge.' I wasn't about to approach the sea lock before finding out more about what lay beyond, a lot more.

A reminder of just how unforgiving the Severn can be I found in the dockworker's club at Sharpness. Newspaper clippings and photographs depicting one of the more recent disasters on the river adorn the club's walls.

Chris Witts knows this side of the Severn's schizophrenic personality all too well. He was a deck boy on tanker barges in the Sixties, trading between Swansea and Worcester, moving between the Severn 'sea' and the Severn 'river.' His pamphlets and talks, *River Severn Tales*, are popular with visitors and tourists to his home town of Gloucester. Chris told me: "Many people have lost their lives on that River, some accidental, some from stupidity. Without a doubt, the most dangerous stretch is also one of the prettiest - from Gloucester to where the Bristol Channel properly begins, at Sharpness."

Chris is right, on both counts. It is hugely attractive country, and a highway virtually alongside that travels from Gloucester west to Chepstow, one of the many Welsh border towns, means the river is accessible to tens of thousands. But even without the 'bore,' the river can be dangerous under even 'normal' conditions. "Fierce tides sweep up this stretch twice a day," Chris warns, "and anyone caught on the sands is certain to drown." So frequent is the threat that a group of

"This is what men have built," wrote sociologist and

novelist Raymond Williams, a native of Wales'

Black Mountains. "Is not everything

then possible?" he asked.

Enough concrete

went into the Second Severn

Crossing to provide a half million

homes with sizeable backyard patios. The

longest bridge in Great Britain, it carries the 'lifeblood of

commerce' through still another important artery of the M-4

motorway connecting Wales with the heart of the country, London and the

Southeast. The fourth historic conquest of the tidal Severn by British engineers, the

structure is an appropriate symbol of the remarkable turn-around of Wales and its once-ailing post-

war economy. The bridge is the proud achievement of an Anglo-French consortium, Laing Construction and

GTM Entrepose. In an era when delays and cost overruns on public projects are commonplace, the two companies

finished the bridge on time and on budget.

volunteers, all experts with vast experience on the river, set up a rescue organisation a few years ago. Their fast boats, 'rigid inflatables,' have saved many lives from their two bases at Beachley on the Welsh side and Sharpness, further upriver on the English shore.

But what about the great mishap I saw portrayed at the docker's club in Sharpness?

"That was the Severn Bridge disaster that happened on the night of 25 October, 1960. Two tanker barges came together in thick fog off Sharpness and drifted into the bridge. They caught fire and exploded, taking a couple of spans of the bridge with them. Five men were killed and the bridge was never re-built."

So, another discovery. The two graceful road bridges that span the Severn today were not the first crossing.

The bridge that ended up in the river in 1960 was there before. Today, if you walk the tow-path alongside the Sharpness Canal, the old abutments that held the bridge can be seen. The rest, what the river didn't take, was demolished. This was an iron bridge completed in 1879 for the Severn and Wye Railway, a structure that carried trains of coal from the mines of the Forest of Dean to Birmingham to the north and Bristol to the south. Like its modern-day counterparts, this bridge was no mean feat of engineering, stretching more than two-thirds of a mile across one of the most formidable parts of the river. As awful as the 1960 incident was, it cannot compare with an earlier disaster, one I came across in my pursuit of more information about the river, in the Gwent Levels. Bordered by rising hills and ridges to the north, these flatlands are the ancient floodplains of the Severn. But little did I know of just how much flooding.

At the tiny hamlet of Peterstone Wentloog, a 15th century church stands on the foundations of a medieval, 12th century structure. It is lucky to be there. On the Northeast corner of the church, a small, unassuming tablet is attached to the stone. It is exactly five feet, six inches above the ground, and it records one of the most terrifying incidents in recorded European history. It tells the observer that this is the height of the sea in the 'Great Flood of 20 January 1606.'

Brian Waters, in his engaging account of his walks along both sides of the Severn, *The Bristol Channel*, says: "This was like no other flood in the history of Britain. This was no river flood, but an invasion of the sea over the sea-wall." More than 2,000 are known to have died, and an area 24 miles long and four miles inland was submerged, that is, almost all of the modern Gwent Levels. Contemporary accounts spoke of 'mighty hills of water,' and it was years before farmers could grow anything in the soil that had been soaked in salt water.

Today, the flood defences along both sides of the Severn are impressive. Many were the engineering work of the world's leading experts on floods, the Dutch. But the levees and dikes, channels and dams built by the US Army Corps of Engineers to tame the mighty Mississippi were equally impressive. Millions of dollars were spent along this vital American waterway in order to make it 'flood-free.' By the Nineties, serious flooding on the Mississippi and its main tributaries was thought of as virtually impossible. And then came the rains of 1993. Within days the river had burst through some of the world's most elaborate and expensive flood defences. Within days, an area four times the size of Wales was inundated, some of the best and most productive farmland in the world. It was the worst

A Great Western InterCity 125 roars out of the century-old Severn Tunnel and into the Welsh countryside as it approaches Cardiff. Running hourly to and from London - a journey of less than two hours - the trains are a far cry from the first railway locomotive, a converted steam engine mounted on what had been a horse-drawn wagon. It also ran in Wales. The year was 1804, and the machine was built by Richard Trevithick, a Cornish engineer working on the pioneering Penydarren Railway near Merthyr Tydfil, the valleys city that gave birth to the Industrial Revolution.

Trevithick's first passengers were two local ironmasters, Samuel Homray and Richard Crawshay, who were joined by a visiting government engineer. Homray and Crawshay were among the world's first industrialists, mining the iron ore that was smelted into the metal, a process that turned the night sky of Merthyr incandescent and created an insatiable demand for an efficient fuel for their furnaces, coal.

Appropriately, a Cardiff University School of Engineering building carries Trevithick's name. Crawshay is remembered only by an obscure Cardiff street bearing his name and the bizarre engraving on his tomb overlooking the steep valleys where he made his vast fortune: "God forgive me."

flood in recorded American history. As one of the rescue workers said at the time, 'We have tornadoes and hurricanes in the States. They strike quickly and are over just as quickly. This was a leisurely disaster.'

Now Americans learned the hard way that trying to tame this vast continental river system was a mistake. Many of the levees will not be re-built. Sadly, neither will many of the communities that the '93 floods destroyed. 'Ol' Miss' will now be allowed to take its natural course.

The threat that rivers the size of the Severn can pose is easily seen. Walk the dikes and levees from Cardiff to Newport. A glance at the sea along any section reveals that at high tide the land protected on the other side is below sea level. The dikes look impressive: massive mounds of earth, rock, concrete and stone. But so were

those along the Mississippi. The Severn, like its American counterpart, is not a river to be taken lightly.

Her Majesty's Coast Guards at Swansea are responsible for that section of the Severn from Sharpness down to Milford Haven that Teranda was to travel. I called them the beautiful August morning we were leaving the Sharpness lock and turning into the Severn. On their 'working' VHF radio channel, I explained our journey and asked for a 'watching brief', sailing jargon for the equivalent of a airline pilot's flightplan. It meant that the Coast Guards would know we were making the trip and would check if we didn't make our 'Estimated Time of Arrival.'

As we emerged from behind the enormous lock-gate, the Severn looked like a sea, a boiling and bubbling one, and I was more than grateful for the opportunity to

A Victo

1879

The bridge that few remember. Built in 1879, ten years before Thomas Walker's tunnel, this 3,700 foot railway bridge 26 miles below the city of Gloucester, was the first to span the notorious tidal stretch of the River Severn. A Victorian engineering masterpiece, it stood until a foggy night in October of 1960 when two tanker barges collided in mid-river and drifted into the abutments before exploding, an incident that cost five sailors their lives.

It was never re-built.

ian engineering masterpiece

follow Raven, an even larger cruiser based at Upton that was making the journey downriver and had invited us to come along. I eagerly accepted since Raven had its own professional skipper, and like Chris Witts, he knew the river forward and backward. It was the 'local knowledge' I had sought and the Admiralty chart advised.

At Sharpness, a boat is about eight nautical miles above the first Severn highway bridge, the one opened in 1969. I had been over it many times. But when it hove into view from the deck of a rolling and pitching cruiser, it was not only a welcome sight but a spectacular one as well. We passed under just at high tide, part of the plan of the Raven's skipper. Now the second crossing was in view, still under construction but with the last span about to be dropped into place. Slipping beneath this towering structure was a truly memorable moment.

Heads craned upwards and squinting in the bright summer sun, all on board gained a new and unforgettable appreciation of what the Severn 'crossings' really mean.

Arriving in Swansea 'roads' hours later, I contacted the Coast Guards and told them of our safe arrival. "Hope you had a pleasant trip," was the reply of the friendly voice that crackled from the radio. "Thanks. You don't know the half of it," I answered.

It had truly been a voyage of discovery.

the lan

the land

land

A 'coal rush' now took place in the valleys of the south. Above all, the two Rhonddas became the 'Black Klondyke.' In 1850 the trout still leapt in the clear waters that ran through the deep woodlands of Llwynypia - the Magpie's Grove. Fifty years later there wasn't a trout or a magpie in the whole deep valley. Long lines of terraced houses choked the lower slopes. The wheels turned day and night over mine shafts dropping their cages over a thousand feet to the lucrative Rhondda No. 3 seam. The endless trains of coal trucks rattled down to the docks at Cardiff and Barry, where the ships of the world crowded the roads to wait their turn at the coal hoists.

This was the real Rape of the Fair Country...

Wynford Vaughan-Thomas
Wales: A History

I'm standing high above the modern Merthyr Tydfil, where the Industrial Revolution is said to have begun, in the tiny hamlet of Faenor, in the graveyard of its equally tiny church. Both look down on the 'terraces' that in the fertile valleys of many countries would be filled with olive groves or rice paddies. Instead there are row upon row of closely-packed houses, the 'little boxes' of song, houses that were hurriedly built in their thousands throughout the valleys of South Wales, thrown up with a minimum of care, cost or attention for miners and their families, mostly in the late 19th century when 'Coal was King.' Little thought and even less imagination went into their design. They were to be cheap and functional and met both criteria. Stretching as far as the eye can see, they line the steep valley walls, row stacked upon row. Separated only by narrow streets and almost backed on to one another except for tiny backyards, they are even today not much sought after, and hence are exceptionally cheap. A century or more after they were built, the communities they comprise are one of the most depressed areas in all of Western Europe. How they could inspire an artist is hard to see, but one, Michael Powell, has made the South Wales Valleys a special object of his work. His 'Terraced Houses,' for example, makes them look almost appealing. The families who first lived in them, and those who remain there today have a different view. Poet Gwyn Thomas, born and raised in such accommodation, would later write that 'never had so little beauty been compressed into so large a space.'

Among the graves in Faenor's church the occasional visitor, or very rare tourist, finds the tomb of Richard Thompson Crawshay, an iron-master whose foundries made him a fortune and were a cog in the wheel of that burst of applied technology that we know as the 'Industrial Revolution.' It is hard to miss, Crawshay's monument to himself, because it is huge. It carries a simple but peculiar inscription: 'God forgive me.' 'Forgive him' for what?, you ask yourself. You need only look around to see why Crawshay pleaded with his maker for pardon, especially in such a public way. How that score was settled we will never know, but at least Crawshay went to his grave with the certain knowledge that God is, after all, in the forgiveness business.

Crawshay was part of that growing, thriving class of 19th century entrepreneurs who infuriated Marx, the bourgeois capitalists he denounced in his brilliant social critique, *Das Kapital*. These were the industrialists who hitched men to the machines that lit the skies of Merthyr and the surrounding valleys with the flames, the red glow of the iron-smelting furnaces that were the crucible for hammering out the metal that history's

The Welsh capital Cardiff and its Bay along the River Severn from space. Clearly visible are the coal-rich valleys to the north and the River Taff. Thanks to the barrage, the Bay is now closed off, and the Atlantic tides that twice each day exposed vast mudflats only a memory.

Wales itself rests on a peninsula that juts into the vast ocean, forming with Cornwall the westernmost extremity of Great Britain. It could fit comfortably into the state of Texas more than 30 times.

The south is gently hilly and eternally green. The remaining half is covered mostly by the Cambrian Mountains. From Mount Snowdon, Britain's highest peak outside Scotland, Ireland can sometimes be glimpsed across the Celtic Sea. All of Great Britain lies north of the fiftieth parallel, well above the border America shares with Canada. Wales owes its maritime climate of highly variable but inevitably mild, misty and very wet weather entirely to the warm waters of the Gulf Stream.

While the geography of Wales remains intact, wave after wave of immigration - mostly from England and Ireland - has changed the human demography of the country forever. Rarely do 'outsiders' complain of ill-treatment by the native Welsh, so ingrained is the Welsh sense of hospitality and just plain good humour. Moreover, like the Bute family from Scotland, the immigrants have also brought notions of enterprise that were alien to the Welsh and made a huge contribution to the region's regeneration.

first modern society required. It was what Welsh writer Jan Morris would later call 'an incandescent enterprise' that left a land 'poisoned by its own exhalations.' This was the beginning of mass manufacturing, the mining and processing of the ore that became iron. Apart from the ostentatious stone that was presumably part of his 'last will and testament,' Crawshay is forgotten, for all of his success. A Cardiff street bears his name, ironically it too lined with a half-dozen modest terraced houses ending in a brewery.

Why did this all take place at Merthyr? A simple answer is because the 'raw' ingredients of the iron industry were there - iron ore, coal and above all, men. Add to the recipe the energy, drive and ambition of men like Crawshay, and you have what today we would call enterprise. But today we would not allow it, having learned the cost, the 'downside,' to use the current jargon of business. In its heyday, it could not have been a pretty sight for all of the riches it meant for Crawshay and others like him. The Scottish historian Thomas Carlyle likened it to a 'vision of hell,' while another Welsh poet Alun Lewis, standing on a neighbouring ridge from Merthyr's a half-century later, surveyed the damage in *The Mountain Over Aberdare*:

> Our stubborn bankrupt village sprawled
> In jaded dusk beneath its nameless hills;
> The drab streets strung across the cwm,
> Derelict workings, tips of slag

In our time, huge efforts have been made to repair and hide the damage. Much of what appears to be part of the natural terrain of the Rhondda Valley, the steep hills rising on either side, are not natural at all. They are literally mountains of 'tip,' a euphemism hiding the reality that they are in fact giant heaps of spoil, the material raised from the earth beneath that was a worthless by-product of mining. I drive up the mountain road behind Merthyr where expensive landscaping has been used to cover the 'tips of slag,' first with topsoil and then grass. It is a odd and queer sort of place, clearly disturbed in some perceptible way that says: 'Here the world was turned inside out.' The earth heals slowly from such terrible wounds, and how long, I ask myself, will it be before the last traces of this upheaval disappear forever?

We can only picture in our minds what Wales might have looked like before Crawshay. A few artists recorded its primeval beauty as did many more poets. It had largely remained untouched since the Ice Age that created it. A country passed over by time and history, Wales held little interest for its English masters, preoccupied as they were with endless wars in Europe, and later their Empire. When change came it was cataclysmic. For beneath this land lay a mineral called

Bowen, Williams, Jenkins, Lloyd, Thomas - and of course - Jones, the most common of all Welsh surnames. Indeed, Jones is so common that many families are known by the occupation of the father: 'Jones the butcher' or 'Jones the baker' or 'Jones the plumber.' Welsh-Americans trying to trace their roots in the Principality face a real challenge since the Welsh appear to have far fewer surnames than virtually any other European nationality. "Why," ask visitors, "is everyone in Wales called Jones?"

Welsh scholars like John and Sheila Rowlands have the answer. It has to do with a practice called 'patronymics' - naming some one after their father's name. This practice went on in Wales for centuries so that after a few generations, a son might be known by a long string of names of his ancestral fathers separated only by 'ap,' the Welsh for 'of.' When forced by census laws to choose a single surname, many of the Welsh looked back over the long list of their ancestors and picked the one they thought was the most prestigious and accomplished.

English surnames, on the other hand, often came from personal names, place names, a feature of the land or an occupation. There was far less scope to do this in a country like Wales where the population was small and scattered in clusters through mostly tiny villages and hamlets, and just about everyone earned their living from the land.

A map of the distribution of surnames in Wales shows the profound impact of the English over the centuries. Many of the traditional Welsh family names were displaced by wave after wave of English invaders or immigrants, leaving the 'native' Welsh more and more confined to the west and north of the country. Even today it is estimated that perhaps nine tenths of the population of Wales would respond to less than 100 different surnames.

Proving how difficult it is to 'keep up with the Jones's,' nearly fourteen per cent of the surnames in Wales are - you guessed it - Jones.

Strategically located on rivers and mountain passes up and down the country are the famous fortresses and castles of Wales. No other area of Europe can boast so many. What was going on here? In a word, centuries of endless conflict. While the rest of medieval Europe was engaged in building commercial centres and cathedrals, the Welsh and their English foes expended much of their energy and fortunes, as well as thousands of lives, on a more or less continuous war for the dominance of a remote and seemingly worthless corner of the British Isles. The two wars King Edward I of England waged against the Welsh in 1277 and 1282 finally ended any hopes of an independent Wales. The conflict was also a highly personal battle between two royal Welsh brothers, Llywelyn, the last native Prince of Wales, and his brother Dafydd, who first sided with the English and then switched his loyalty back to his brother when King Edward did not reward his treachery. In the end, their armies were overrun by the English and the heads of both brothers ended up on pikes outside the Tower of London.

The most significant dates in Welsh history are almost invariably associated with one uprising after another intended to thwart England's determined domination. By the end of Edward's wars with the Welsh princes, the English were so firmly established that the tradition of naming the monarch's successor the 'Prince of Wales' was begun. That practice continues to this day. In 1969, Queen Elizabeth's eldest son, Charles, was made Prince of Wales in an elaborate ceremony within the walls of the magnificent Caernarvon Castle where every male successor to the throne has been invested with the same title since King Edward's son took it in 1301. This is why Wales is also known in Great Britain as a 'Principality.'

Largely dormant for the next five-hundred years, Welsh nationalism was revived in the nineteenth century, swept up in the fervour of a European-wide movement to forge nations out of some perceived national identity. Across the continent cultural societies combed tirelessly through history to find the tiniest justification for a 'new' Czechoslovakia, Ireland, Flanders, Serbia, Croatia or Wales. What they couldn't substantiate in ancient archives they largely invented, creating enduring and endearing legends out of such myths as the story of King Arthur. The past of nations, like people themselves, are a mixture of fact and fantasy. Where our memories fail us, where facts are in short supply, we often resort to the imagination. In Wales, the boundary between myth and history is now irretrievably blurred, and legend has been piled upon legend in an accretion of layers like the sedimentary rock that makes up so much of its mountains. In both fact and fiction there remains a consistent theme: the romantic notion of the Welsh as the oppressed, the victims of a war-like neighbour.

This is why anti-English feelings surface periodically in Wales, right up to the present, and sometimes has been more than a little bad-tempered. While never reaching the proportions of a Northern Ireland, Welsh nationalists have none the less made life difficult for the English on more than one occasion. When Margaret Thatcher was campaigning to become Britain's first woman prime minister, she promised the Welsh their own television channel to augment the few hours of Welsh-language programming on the BBC. When she arrived at 10 Downing Street months later, she seemed to backtrack on the commitment. Her equivocation resulted in the bombing of several BBC transmitters in Wales and the vow by a prominent Welsh poet to starve himself to death. The result was the creation of Sianel Pedwar Cymru, a television channel devoted to Welsh language and culture.

Historically, the English have totally dominated the other 'nations' of the United Kingdom from their capital, London. So pervasive is London's influence in every area of British life that one could argue that Britain is not a country with a capital, but a capital with a country.

Today there seems little danger that the Welsh will join the other 'lost tribes' of pre-historic Europe. What Prince Llywelyn and other Welsh patriots could not achieve by force may now come about through politics. Armed with a narrow victory in a 1997 referendum for devolution, Welsh nationalists now have their first legislative body since the middle ages. While its powers are limited, especially in comparison to the Scottish Parliament or any American state assembly or legislature, it is still a historic step toward self-government and perhaps eventually, independence. Champions of the notion of a Welsh nation point to neighbouring Ireland as a model, similar in population if not larger in size. But like the British Isles themselves, that island is also divided, with the six counties of Northern Ireland thus far remaining firmly in the United Kingdom.

The cultural and linguistic patchwork quilt of Europe is paradoxically enriching and burdensome at the same time. The dreams of the founders of the European Community, those who would erase Europe's much fought-over boundaries, must still cope with what Scottish journalist Neal Ascherson has called "the most powerful source of political magic on earth - nationalism."

coal, the material geologists define as a 'black or brown carbonaceous rock consisting of layers of partially decomposed vegetation deposited in the Carboniferous period.' Man had known about it at a time we lived in caves. These layers, or 'seams,' frequently broke through the surface, and even primitive tribes quickly learned that coal would burn, producing fierce heat with little smoke. But it wasn't until the 'Age of Industry,' and the need for metals on a vast scale that much attention was paid to this inconsequential rock. Now it had value, enough so that it was systematically mined.

Not since the geological upheavals of pre-historic times, the forces that created the very minerals Crawshay and others sought, had Wales experienced such turbulence. At the very time that nearby Cardiff remained an unremarkable settlement, largely confined within its medieval walls, Merthyr boomed. Looking at the two cities today, it is hard to believe that as late as 1861, when the census of that year showed Cardiff was beginning to slip its bonds of insignificance as a modest and unimportant market town, its population paled beside that of Merthyr. Gone was the 'Sabbath stillness' of an earlier time. The long, sinewy valley of the Rhondda that stretched some sixteen miles and never exceeded a mile in width, was teeming with an extraordinary 115,000 souls, 40,000 of them miners working in 50 pits. By the end of the first decade of the 20th century, Wales could boast of an astonishing 250,000 men working in the coal fields alone, a level of intensity that attracted tens of thousands of immigrants, for a short time more than were to emigrate to the 'New World' across the expanse of the Atlantic.

If nations kept ledgers as carefully as the bookkeepers of the coal barons, few would quarrel that the costs outweighed the short-lived benefits. They dug for coal as if there were no tomorrow, as if it and the 'prosperity' it brought would last forever. For decades, Merthyr was the most intensively mined area in the world. What it cost in human terms however, today beggars belief. Every *six hours* a miner was killed while working the seams of the 'Black Klondyke.' Every *two minutes* one was injured. The toll above ground was equally shocking. Because the waters of the River Taff were diverted to drive steam engines, the river became an open sewer and outbreaks of cholera and typhoid were frequent. By the middle of the 19th century, 60 per cent of all burials in Merthyr Tydfil were of children under the age of five.

But even these outrages were overshadowed by periodic mining disasters that extracted a terrible price.. I relate to you only two of many. In the 1913 Senghennydd tragedy alone, 439 men died. Sixty were less than twenty years old, and eight were boys of fourteen. One woman, already a widow, lost all three sons; another, her husband and both sons.

Let us not be so insensitive as to compare the grief and loss of one community with another. Nevertheless, the mere mention of Aberfan still evokes a wincing pain. I am in another graveyard. And not since I first stood in the neatly cropped and meticulously attended cemeteries behind the Normandy invasion beaches, have I been so deeply moved. At Normandy, where thousands of Allied soldiers died to free Europe of Nazi tyranny, the precise rows of crosses span one's entire field of view - in every direction. Aberfan's resting place is a miniature in size, but not in impact. For here, in tiny graves, 116 children are buried, classmates who died together at the school that once stood near-by, at the

Wales is at the forefront of one of the most important economic and political developments of our time. Taking advantage of the globilization of countless multi-national companies on the one hand, and the increasing political and economic unity of Europe on the other, the country has aggressively sought out foreign investment. In 1976, the UK government set up the Welsh Development Agency and gave it the challenging task of regenerating the Principality's economy in the wake of the decline of its traditional 'smokestack' industries of coal, iron and steel.

In 1983, the Agency began a concerted campaign of luring overseas companies to Wales. Today it rightly boasts that 1,800 inward investment projects have yielded £11.8 billion and created and safeguarded 175,000 jobs in one of the most economically depressed areas in Europe where wages are still relatively low.

The WDA's success has been widely hailed, much envied, and repeatedly copied not only in Britain but throughout Europe, especially in areas that also suffered from the decline of native industries. With just over three million people, Wales accounts for only six per cent of Great Britain's total population, yet has attracted the overwhelming bulk of foreign investment in the past two decades. Some argue that this dependence on foreign companies has made Wales a 'branch economy' where important decisions about the future of the Principality are made elsewhere. The Agency's champions respond by saying that its work has changed the face of Wales from an image of militant poverty portrayed in Richard Llewellyn's *How Green Was My Valley*, to a modern manufacturing-based economy based on the investment of dozens of the world's leading corporations. As the Financial Times noted in a recent editorial, "However much the individual Welsh have made a mark on the world, it is not in Wales's collective nature to be a pioneer." It is highly doubtful that the paper will reach that same conclusion in ten years time.

Today, tourism is the most rapidly growing 'industry' in Wales, and small wonder. One American couple, who were making their fourth journey to Wales, told me: "We keep coming back because once you have been here, this country seems to have its foot in your door forever."

foot of a giant mound of rain-soaked spoil. On an October morning in 1966, the 'mountain' behind the school began to move, first slowly and then, according to the helpless witnesses who watched, with frightening and terrifying speed. Within seconds it had engulfed the school, tonnes of black ooze that crushed everything in its path. A heartbroken world responded, and £151,000 was collected for this tiny, devastated community where nearly every family lost a daughter, a son, a cousin, nephew or niece. But it wasn't until 1996,

Part of a mosaic of European languages, Welsh is spoken by only one in five of the more than three million people who call Wales home. The language has survived in spite of deliberate attempts to discourage its use, a misguided policy of many Welsh schools that for years believed that Welsh could be of no practical use outside Wales. While that policy has long been discarded, what is remarkable is that Welsh continues to exist alongside the most powerful and pervasive language in the world, English.

"Full hearts and empty vessels" is the way Welsh writer and journalist Dylan Iorwerth describes the dilemma of his native tongue. Since 1963, Cymdeithas yr Iaith - the most powerful pressure group on behalf of the language - has deployed every tactic from sit-ins to burglary to advance the cause of the language. Their campaign culminated in a Welsh Language Act, passed in 1993, creating a statutory body to advise the British government on Welsh language matters. Another success - reversing the discrimination against Welsh speakers that was official British government policy for much of the 19th century - is its revival in schools where thousands of children now have the opportunity of learning Welsh along with their routine studies of English.

Still another positive move forward is Prime Minister Tony Blair's commitment to 'devolution,' a move that will give Wales a national assembly and Scotland a parliament. In Wales, the assembly will deliberate in both English and Welsh, another boost to a language once in danger of disappearing altogether.

Ironically, Wales has no newspaper of significant circulation that publishes in the language. But it does have S4C, Sianel Pedwar Cymru, literally the 'Welsh fourth channel,' a Welsh language TV outlet funded through advertising and public subsidy that has provided a new impetus for the language.

Champions of the language however can become a little overzealous. I recently stood behind a Welsh speaker checking out her weekly shopping at a large Cardiff supermarket. She insisted on conducting the transaction in Welsh even though - like all Welsh speakers - she was perfectly capable in English as well. Ironically, the frustrated but polite and accommodating girl behind the cash register later told me that she too was Welsh, as were generations of her family, but none were Welsh speaking. There are other, perhaps more disturbing trends. Turning history on its head, some city councils in traditional Welsh-speaking areas now stand accused of discriminating against English speakers by insisting that those applying for jobs in local government be able to work in Welsh. In another instance, one council argued for years whether Welsh should appear above or below English on traffic signs. There are countless examples, and the 'Letters to the Editor' columns of virtually every newspaper in Wales provide a regular battleground for those from both camps to confront one another.

Few issues are more divisive in modern Wales than the language. In the end, the resurgence of the language is bound to throw up minor inconveniences for those who are not bilingual. The real question is: Would the world be richer or poorer if Welsh culture and the Welsh language were to disappear?

Europe provides countless other examples of minority languages, from Frisian in The Netherlands to Basque in Spain. Each has had to fight, sometimes literally, to avoid being overwhelmed by the language of the majority. Dylan Iorwerth, sums up the problem succinctly: "Is a language to be nurtured through statute or through a spirit which often flourishes on the oxygen of rebellion?"

thirty years later, that the money reached the bereaved, without interest. The media across Britain treated it as a scandal, and scandalous it was. The Welsh Office, the representation of Her Majesty's Government in Wales, had diverted the money to removing what was left of the slag heap that was the responsibility of managers of Aberfan's mine. But such mines no longer belonged to the Crawshays of Wales; in a cruel twist of fate they belonged to the public, nationalised in a fury of socialist fervour following World War II when Britain's Conservatives, led by Churchill, were unceremoniously thrown out of office and replaced by Labour, and the promised welfare state. As American President Harry S Truman once remarked, "The only thing new in the world is the history you don't know."

We know today, and stand here long enough, and one could become very angry or very disconsolate. This is after all, a small and close community's heartfelt monument to a generation of its children and the 28 adults who died with them. But who to blame? There is blame enough to spread across those of any political belief. The reign of 'King Coal' left behind a wasteland. Richard Llewellyn poignantly summed up the price in *How Green Was My Valley*: 'There is a patience in the Earth to allow us to go into her, and dig and hurt with tunnels and shafts.' On my desk as I write stands a wooden plinth with a piece of anthracite, the hard coal that fuelled the steam-producing engines that drove much of the Industrial Revolution, including thousands of ships. I brought it up from a mine in North Wales near the tiny town of Rhos, near Wrexham. Writing an article on the world-wide decline of the coal industry 20 years ago for the Cincinnati Enquirer, I accompanied a shift of Welsh miners to the Gresham pit for the night. It was a sobering experience, and this souvenir that I

Mae hen wlad fy nhadau yn annwyl i mi
Gwlad beirdd a chantorion enwogion o fri
Ei gwrol ryfelwr, gwlad garwyr tra mad
Tros ryddid collasant eu gwaed.

Gwlad Gwlad
Pleidiol wyf i'm gwlad
Tra môr yn fur i'r bur hoff bau
O bydded i'r hen iaith barhau

Land of my fathers, O land of the free
A land of poets and minstrels, famed men
Her brave warriors, patriots much blessed
It was for freedom that they lost their blood

Wales! Wales!
I am devoted to my country
So long as the sea is a wall to this fair land
May the ancient language remain

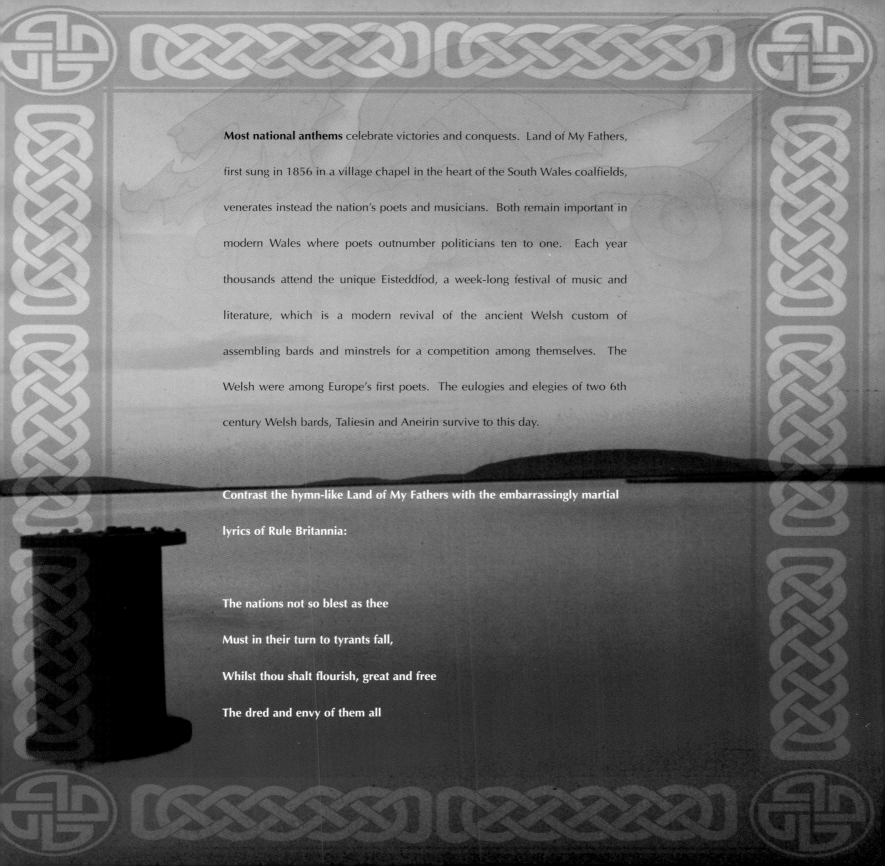

Most national anthems celebrate victories and conquests. Land of My Fathers, first sung in 1856 in a village chapel in the heart of the South Wales coalfields, venerates instead the nation's poets and musicians. Both remain important in modern Wales where poets outnumber politicians ten to one. Each year thousands attend the unique Eisteddfod, a week-long festival of music and literature, which is a modern revival of the ancient Welsh custom of assembling bards and minstrels for a competition among themselves. The Welsh were among Europe's first poets. The eulogies and elegies of two 6th century Welsh bards, Taliesin and Aneirin survive to this day.

Contrast the hymn-like Land of My Fathers with the embarrassingly martial lyrics of Rule Britannia:

The nations not so blest as thee

Must in their turn to tyrants fall,

Whilst thou shalt flourish, great and free

The dred and envy of them all

brought up reminded me that every time I switched on a light or ran an appliance, it was because these men had made it possible.

One of the many thousands was B. L. Coombes, a miner and then later a writer. Coombes told of the fear and the wretched, exhausting work in *My First Night Underground*, where he and his mates we working a coal seam only 36 inches high. Try crawling in the dark in front of your kitchen cabinets which are about the same height, imagining six inches of icy water on the floor and thick dust filling the air. Few of us would envy them their jobs, regardless of the pay.

> Our place was going continually downhill. Every three yards forward took us downward another yard. It was heavy climbing to go back, and every shovelful of coal or stone had to be thrown uphill. Water was running down the roadway to us and an electric pump was gurgling away on our right side. We were always working in about six inches of water, and if the

pump stopped or choked for ten minutes the coal was covered with water. There is nothing pleasant about water underground. It looks so black and sinister. It makes every move uncomfortable and every stroke with the mandril splashes the water about your body.

Another entry in our ledger of costs and benefits of the Black Klondyke. The ruptured, torn and scarred face of the land was not the only legacy.

Years before I visited Spain, James Michener's engaging account of his travels there, *Iberia*, helped prepare me for what I would see in a land he learned to love. He wrote: "I have long believed than any man interested in either the mystic or romantic aspects of life must sooner or later define his attitude concerning Spain." He was right, and he could have written similar words about the Welsh. There is something especially poignant about romantics who never realise their dreams, about a defeated people. The dry, barren almost desert-like landscape of Andalusia, neglected and exploited by Spain's rulers, produced Garcia Federico Lorca and his ethereal and mystic poetry, masterpieces like *Romancero gitano*. It also produced an inevitable and predictable generation of revolutionaries: Spain's most fervent Communists. Led by Lorca and accompanied by hundreds of volunteers from Britain, including Wales, they spreadheaded the attack on the "facistas" of General Franco in the civil war whose outcome was equally predictable. They lost. And just as one senses the melancholy behind the facade of the "pueblo blancos" of modern-day Andalusia, the valleys of South Wales evoke a similar feeling: here something went badly wrong, and the scars are yet to heal. Here and in Spain, there remains to this day a complex legacy.

Leader writers in establishment London newspapers of the 1930s wrote scathing denunciations of the 'Red Rhondda,' not understanding why miners from this famous coal-mining valley and countless others up and down Wales organised into trade unions, and quickly affiliated themselves with the only movement of their era that appeared to offer hope and sustenance: socialism. Many became Communists, and many became folk heroes as members of the International Brigade in the Spain's Civil War; Fascists anywhere were their enemies too.

George Steiner, the British cultural historian, has written that the 19th century was characterised by 'a trust in the unfolding excellence of fact.' The value of progress, both personal and social, was unquestioned. Men swept up in the increasing belief that science held every answer, like Charles Darwin and his theories of evolution, were slowly undermining centuries of belief in Christianity. But read Marx, a child of this age if there

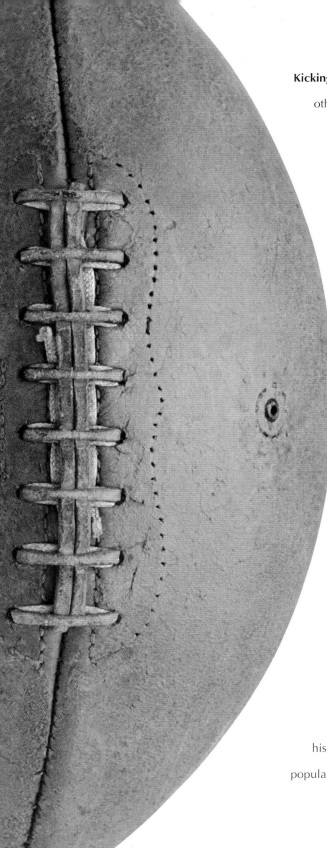

Kicking a ball around a field must be one of the oldest pastimes known to mankind. But it was an otherwise forgotten a pupil at one of England's most exclusive private schools for boys who gave the ancient sport a new twist. He is forever remembered by a modest plaque in the Rugby School Close that reads:

> William Webb Ellis, who with a fine disregard for the rules of football as played in his time, first took the ball in his arms and ran with it.
>
> AD 1823

How a game born on the school playing fields of an elite school founded in 1567 came to the valleys of industrial Wales centuries later is a matter of conjecture. Eddie Butler, himself a former captain of Pontypool and Wales, and now the Rugby correspondent of the London Observer, says "It was violent; it was poetic, and the better the Welsh became at it, the more it grew into an expression of defiance aimed at the gentlemen-masters of the forges and the mines, and above all the English."

It could be compared to bullfighting where no quarter is asked and none given. Unlike American football, where the players appear in more armour than a medieval knight, the gladiators of Rugby are clad in only T-shirts and shorts. Veterans of the sport are easily spotted, not just because of their imposing proportions, but from the permanently bent noses and scars they wear like badges of honour.

In 1871, decades after Ellis had picked up the ball that day in Rugby School, the sport became recognised officially, by being outlawed. Britain's Football Association, proponents and protectors of soccer, ruled that handling the ball was illegal. But it was too late, and the two sports parted company for all time. Little could young Ellis know that his imaginative departure from the rules that afternoon would spawn one of the world's most popular sports, and no where is it played with more ferocity and determination than in Wales.

Years ago, a driver stopped to ask me directions along Cardiff's River Taff across from the National Stadium, the Welsh 'cathedral' to Rugby.

"Is that the National Stadium?" he asked.

"Yup."

"Can you get inside?" he continued.

"Sure, there's a museum too."

"You mean I can walk on the pitch?"

"I think they allow that," I replied.

His wife sat slowly shaking her head. "This is a pilgrimage for him," she told me, cradling his video camera on her lap. "He wants to stand on the grass where someone called Gareth Edwards played."

When the old structure came down to make way for the new 72,500 seat Millennium Stadium, this Rugby zealot from the other side of Britain was no doubt one of the many fans who lined up to buy a square foot of the turf, grass that the legendary Edwards and other warriors of Wales nurtured with their sweat and occasionally, blood.

Like so many projects across modern Europe today, the stadium is an international effort with manufacturers in Spain, Belgium and Italy supplying everything from one of the world's largest cranes to the retractable roof. Many of the hundreds of men racing the clock to finish the structure in time for Rugby's equivalent of baseball's 'World Series', are the same steel erectors, scaffolders, welders and labourers who defied the awesome River Severn to build its second crossing for John Laing plc, contractors for this £121 million pound project.

One of them is Steve Cunliffe, a 'Laing man' as he describes himself, who has been with the company for more than three decades. From far off Lancashire in England's north, Steve is a graduate engineer who has been with the company for 32 years. He has the formidable task of making certain each of thousands of parts arrive on schedule, and that they will fit where they belong. Is he a Rugby fanatic? I ask. "No, my passion is golf," he replies. But he does use the new Second Severn Crossing, and he helped build that too.

was ever one, and you will hear undeniable echoes of the visions of Isaiah and later, even Christ and his Apostles. It was Christianity without the trappings. Workers every where had only to see their common purpose, only climb one more mountain, make only one more sacrifice.

It is easy today to forget how much hope Communism offered to the victims of the Industrial Revolution. There are countless monuments, buildings and even cities named in honour of the men who walked away with the prizes of the Industrial Revolution, the riches that coal and iron produced. Sadly, there are few to the men and women who carried the burden, the back-breaking work in either Wales, Spain or anywhere else outside the old Soviet Union where workers' achievements were hypocritically celebrated by statues in every square of every city, while at the very same time the commissars assumed the power and privileges once enjoyed only by czars.

As a graft on the body politic, Communism failed to 'take' in Britain, but it did inspire the creation of the first unions of miners, and later, the Labour Party itself. The miners of Wales were central to both.

In the 1900 General Election, Scotsman Keir Hardie was elected by the voters of Merthyr Tydfil as the first Labour member of Parliament. A miner who admired the writings of the American revolutionary Thomas Paine, author of *The Rights of Man*, Hardie was also influenced by Marx, and especially Christ. In his 1907 book, *From Serfdom to Socialism*, he wrote: "The impetus which drove me first into the Labour movement, and the inspiration which has carried me on in it, has been derived more from the teachings of

Jesus of Nazareth than from all other sources combined."

By 1906, Labour had 29 seats in Parliament, and the 1910 General Election saw 40 elected to the House of Commons. One of history is greatest champions of the common man, Hardie almost single-handedly launched the trade union movement in the coalfields as well, and by the end of the Second War, the National Union of Mineworkers counted 533,000 members in its ranks.

At last the story of the story of these everyday people is beginning to emerge. I find one at the unique South Wales Coalfield Collection and the South Wales Miners' Library, both splendidly housed at University of Wales in Swansea. Scholars there began in 1969 to collect and display the artefacts of the social, political and industrial turmoil that swept through the coalfields of South Wales in the first few decades of the 20th century. It is worth seeing, and of all the vast material assembled, nothing demonstrates the faith the miners felt in their ability to act together more than their banners.

There are thirty-nine in all, twenty-seven from the National Union of Mineworkers lodges, including one from the Krasnaya Presna Working Women brought back from the Union of Soviet Socialist Republics to Wales in 1927. Another is from Abercraf Lodge, closed in 1967, and translated from the Welsh reads: 'Workers of the world unite for peace and socialism.' Two miners are pictured, one white and one coloured, although the helpful librarian explains that the second miner is more likely to be Spanish than black since many Spaniards left their own country to find work in the Welsh mines.

Although William Webb Ellis, the Rugby schoolboy who broke the rules to launch the sport may have been long forgotten, the children of Ysgol Gymraeg Treganna School in Wales are sure of their own place in the future of the sport. They buried a time capsule in the new stadium now marked by an engraved plaque. And what will an archaeologist find when he unearths it thousands of years from now? The school's football T-shirt, a CD and a yo-yo.

Wales is a land where myth and legend have become inseparable from facts and history. Take the film *Zulu*, for example. The 1963 Hollywood depiction of one of the most desperate moments in the history of the British Army celebrates the impossible stand of a tiny garrison of 84 soldiers, part of Company B of the 2nd Battalion of the 24th Regiment, against the onslaught of an estimated 4,000 Zulu warriors. The film not only boosted the career of London-born actor Michael Caine, but it also gave rise to the belief that the men who defended 'Rorke's Drift' on January 22, 1879,

were mostly Welsh, members of the South Wales Borderer, a regiment that to this day makes its headquarters in the mountain town of Brecon not far from Cardiff.

Rorke's Drift did happen. And the unbending courage in the face of terrifying odds shown that day in South Africa by those men is also a fact. But only a handful were Welsh. There was no 'South Wales Borderers' regiment. That was a later creation, part of the periodic re-shuffling of a vast imperial army. Nor did they stand on the

ramparts and sing *Men of Harlech* in response to a Zulu war chant.

Those men, English, Irish and Welsh, were all part of the 24th Warwickshire Regiment of Foot, which in the 19th century also made Brecon its headquarters. What they achieved that day was a kind of immortality, the award of the Victoria Cross to more soldiers than any engagement of British forces in any war before or since — and accurate or not — a place in the pantheon of Welsh heroes, real and imagined.

Each of the banners expresses militant hope, pleas for unity, and recalls our innocent, unalloyed belief that there is only one more hill to climb beyond which lies a workers' paradise.

In reality what lay beyond was grinding disappointment and disillusion. While it may be difficult to pinpoint the beginning of the coal industry in Wales, it is easy to mark its end. The strike of 1984-85, an action that embraced mines across Britain, was the watershed. How can I be so precise? A simple statistic tells the story. March of 1984 marked the beginning of a strike by nearly every coal-miner in Britain. On the day they began to walk off their jobs, 191,000 were employed in 170 mines across the country, nearly half of them in Wales alone. When it finished a year later, a mere 10,000 miners were left working in what remained of their industry -

a mere 17 pits.

For sheer bitterness, violence and virtually open warfare, Americans would have to think back to the labour upheavals of the 1930s. Police fought miners, miners fought each other, neighbour fought neighbour, even innocent members of the public were injured, and in one instance killed. Watching it as a journalist, one could be forgiven thinking that British democracy itself was in peril. The outcome was never in doubt. The miners, led nationally by the provocative and belligerent Arthur Scargill - who had correctly predicted the intentions of his sworn enemy, Prime Minister Margaret Thatcher to close down the industry - were more than decimated. Their industry, and with it a way of life, was simply wiped out. As another journalist, Dave Hill of The Guardian, would write a decade after the strike,

It is not only touching but essential that the strike should be so keenly remembered. This is not because every participant was an utterly unblemished socialist saint. It is because, when the balance sheet is totalled, the striking miners, their families and friends represented a version of British life that is a thousand times more generous than that preferred by those who set out to destroy them.

'Touching' is the word. There is a scene in the film version of Richard Llewellyn's *How Green is My Valley*, of miners in a fictitious Welsh village marching arm-in-arm to their pit, their voices raised in a rallying anthem. I watched an identical scene in Maerdy in March of 1985. One of the 'Little Moscows' of the South Wales valleys, Maerdy's miners had held out until desperate, some even said hungry. But when they knew that their year-long struggle was over, they returned to work *en masse*, singing as they went, their voices bouncing and echoing off the valley walls. Beatrix Campbell, a journalist from London's Independent newspaper, recalls the comment of an Irishman who helped organise the parade-like atmosphere surrounding the march back: 'Maerdy represents that Celtic thing about knowing how to handle defeat. Defeat is one of the things the Welsh, the Scots and the Irish know how to do.'

For all its poignancy, for all its truly terrible costs in human and environmental terms, there was a totally unexpected beneficiary. Part of the legacy, the one important entry on the 'plus' side of this tear-stained ledger, is the city of Cardiff.

dazzling cluster of civic buildings

the city

the city
dazzling cluster of civic buildings

I saw the cities of many men,

and learned their manners.

Homer, *The Odyssey*

The Severn Sea, the land of Wales, the city of Cardiff, and its ocean bay. To encompass it all requires a unique viewing point, what Shakespeare called a 'coign of vantage.' Drive north from Cardiff up what the locals call Caerphilly 'mountain,' and you find just that spot: a sweeping panorama that in an instant provides the framework for understanding such a large and important segment of Welsh history. Face the north and you look down on the town of Caerphilly itself. There below is one of Europe's most striking castles, a medieval fortress with a leaning tower more precariously balanced than Pisa's. On the horizon is the outline of the highest mountains in south Wales, the Brecon Beacons. To the east and west, the parallel valleys whose buried black treasure was torn from the earth and sent south to the sea by every conveyance. Wheel about and face the sun. Looking south there is the city that came to dominate virtually everything in sight but the land across the Severn Sea, England.

Apart from the city itself the scene is almost overwhelmed by the majesty of the Severn. Here it is no longer a river but a wide and untamed estuary of the open Atlantic a few miles to the west. Flatholm and Steepholm, islands that still carry the names given them by Viking invaders centuries ago, are in the foreground. The winding River Taff, whose name provides every Welshman with the label 'Taffy,' here empties into the Severn and helps form the 'bite' from the land once known as 'Tiger Bay.'

In less than a century the city that sprawls before you grew from an insignificant backwater to one of the most important and prosperous ports of the world - and then went into an almost terminal decline. Historians would probably argue that it was World War Two that gave Cardiff breathing space and arrested the slide into economic oblivion. Miners were excused from military duty during that conflict, and small wonder. The munitions factories of Britain could not have functioned without coal. But that same need also made the coalports of the Severn a tantalising target for Germany's Luftwaffe, an objective made even more crucial when the build-up for the invasion of France was underway.

Bristol, England's most important Severn port, was obliterated along with its harbour city, Avonmouth. Swansea, Wales 'second city' and a long-time rival of Cardiff, was similarly hammered. Dafydd Rowlands, a Welsh writer who was raised in Swansea, recalled the terror in his story, *A Child's War,* where the morning after a German raid, he and his school mates would collect jagged bits of shrapnel on their way to school, "the cold remnants of a hot night."

Both Swansea and Bristol were essentially re-built in the years following 1945. Walk through each city and the 'patches' show. Not so in Cardiff, a city that was largely spared the agony that turned the East End of London into a vista of rubble and virtually made cities like Portsmouth and Plymouth, strategic ports on the English Channel, unrecognisable to those lucky inhabitants who survived years of the blitz.

There were casualties in Cardiff, of course, both civic and personal. The city's charming and ancient Llandaff

Cathedral, a priceless amalgam of centuries of Gothic construction, was nearly destroyed although the visitor would hardly know today, so painstaking was the repair. Any building, including a cathedral, can be re-built given sufficient time and money. Not so with the human victims.

Whatever else it did, the upheaval that we know as World War Two gave Cardiff another chance. While Swansea and Bristol faced the colossal task of rebuilding almost from the ground up, Cardiff was relatively untouched. It had been catapulted from minor cross-roads to a major port in the span of a century or less. The decline of coal and the Great Depression of the 1930s seemed to mark an end to its brief luminance. The war was as unwelcome as it was useless in restoring Cardiff's economy to the level of prosperity it enjoyed at the height of the coal boom. The slow return into the obscurity from which it had emerged 150 years earlier seemed destined to continue.

Why? Largely because the Welsh seemed unable to exploit the opportunity that coal provided, and when the best seams were exhausted, or no longer profitable to mine, there was little to fall back on. The danger of relying almost exclusively on coal was evident at the time. In 1907, a decade before he was to become Prime Minister of the country, David Lloyd George told the Cardiff business community that "you have obtained all your prosperity from the superiority of your mineral wealth." He pointed to Scotland as an example that Wales should emulate. "Go to the Tyne; go to the Clyde and there you will find that success is due to the superiority of workmanship, superiority of brain."

Writer Jan Morris explains this characteristic of the Welsh by saying the "Welshman's living has generally been elemental. He doesn't make or manufacture things, but grows them, or gets them or takes them somewhere, and sells them when he can."

Lord Butes, ironically all Scots. While both were largely benign governors, Rome regarded Wales largely as a border outpost and not worth serious exploitation. The Bute's, canny in business and politics, were far more astute, amassing one of the greatest fortunes in

Descended from the royal house of Scotland's Stuart's, the 2nd Marquess of Bute included in his vast fortunes not only the family's ancestral home on the Isle of Bute in Scotland, but Cardiff itself. Most of the city was part of his Welsh estates, and there was little of value in South Wales that he did not own or control. The family were landlords over 20,000 homes in Cardiff alone; owned half of the coalfields in the valleys above the city; financed and operated the port that received millions of tons of coal for shipment every year; and much of the railway network that supported the industry. The picturesque St John's Church in the middle of Cardiff was essentially his private chapel. The Town Clerk of the city conveniently was his property agent, and for good measure, he also owned the city's daily newspaper.

All of this was to be inherited by his son, the 3rd Marquess. An eccentric by any definition, he shocked Victorian Britain by becoming a convert to Catholicism, as well as a controversial

opponent of blood sports. His love of art and architecture was unlimited, if sometimes of questionable taste. A patron to dozens of architects in Scotland and Wales, the 3rd Marquess transformed Cardiff Castle into a Gothic 'wedding cake,' dividing his time between it and his even more lavish Mount Stuart estate on the Isle of Bute. Altogether, the family's Welsh and Scottish estates covered more than 117,000 acres.

By the end of the war, the Bute's had lost interest in Wales. Their investments in coal and shipping had yielded them a vast fortune, but both were now in decline. Upon succeeding his late father in 1947, the 5th Marquess gave Cardiff Castle and its extensive grounds to the city and retired to Scotland. The present Marquess is better known as 'Johnny Dumfries,' a former racing driver who was the British Formula Three Champion in 1984, and the joint winner of Le Mans in 1988.

What Lloyd George didn't say that day in Cardiff was that Wales was still regarded as a colony. There was little difference between the rule of the Romans and the rule of the English, and their Procurators, the successive

history. The Romans took gold from the mountains of mid-Wales; the Bute's extracted coal from the valleys of the South.

The Bute family gave more than their fortune to Cardiff. One of the many statues in Cathays Park commemorates Lord Ninian Edward Crichton Stuart, one of three sons of the eccentric 3rd Marquess. After serving in Parliament, Stuart was killed in action during the Battle of Loos in 1915, a 32-year-old lieutenant in the Welch Regiment of the Territorials. He is one of the more than 35,000 young men of Wales who died in World War I. Not far from his memorial is the stately Temple of Peace where their sacrifice is recalled. The names of all are inscribed in the 1,100 pages of a 'Book of Remembrance.' Each day at 11 o'clock, the time of the armistice that ended the war on 11 November 1919, a page is turned.

Today, the legacy of the Romans is barely discernible. They left no grand amphitheatres or temples, only forts and the occasional villa of a minor politician or army officer. The Bute's, on the other hand, literally built a city as a monument to themselves and their allies, the coal barons.

Cathays Park. By the mid-19th century, the city had run out of room to grow, hemmed in on the south by the shallow marshes where the Taff spilled into the Severn, and to the north by the sprawling estates of Lord Bute. Much of his land was an enormous, carefully manicured park stretching both sides of the river, part of the grounds of his castle. A second, even larger plot was

An interesting and sometimes revealing way to think of cities is to compare them to living things themselves. Cities are almost organic in this sense They grow, extend, develop - and not infrequently - decline. The Welsh scholar and social critic, Raymond Henry Williams, saw cities this way, living, evolving organisms. Williams made it central to his engaging book, *The Country and the City*, written partly while he was a visiting professor at California's Stanford University. Look at a highway map of Britain or any other developed country and you will see what Williams meant when he observed that "The concentrated city is in the process of being replaced by what is in effect a transport network: the conurbation, the city region, the London-Birmingham axis." He saw this as perhaps a final development for cities as they become essentially "a province or even a state."

Raymond Williams, like so many Welsh in the 20th century, spent most of his adult life away from Wales. Like the thousands that fled

the mining valleys, Williams and countless other bright, ambitious and determined young people saw their future elsewhere. In most instances, such a haemorrhage of talent and ability might mark the beginning of terminal decline. But there is a kind of 'genetic loop' built into the Welsh psyche, a magnetic urge that draws them back, or even if they remain in exile prompts them to always fight the 'Welsh corner.' Moreover there is a indomitable spirit among these people, a kind of resilience that bubbles up when the going gets tough. Although nearly extinguished, it was resurrected to become an antidote to Cardiff's seemingly irreversible decline, and would surface in a visionary plan for its desolated and mostly deserted dockland. It would change the sceptical and even cynical outlook of a generation, and ignite another burst of civic energy, like that which created the city's stunning Cathays Park. Tracing the origin of that spark is a story in itself.

The manifestation of their pride, their vision, their determination, not to mention their money - was

really a huge heath that the Bute family had enclosed early in the century. It stretched from the edge of the city miles to the north, ending at the 'foothills' of Caerphilly Mountain.

Only Bute himself could resolve the dilemma. It was, after all, his funding of the first dock that helped create the coal boom, and the rapid expansion of Cardiff that followed. An approach in 1859 to Bute's agents - he was still a minor - was initially rejected. In 1873 another offer was turned down. Even a proposal to use a parcel of it for a memorial commemorating Queen Victoria's Jubilee was ignored. The attitude of the town and the town council toward the Bute family, according to Cardiff historian Edward Chappell, veered in those days from "gross servility to intense hostility." And when Bute stubbornly stuck to a price of £158,000 for 58 acres of his land, a heated and lengthy debate was touched off that only ended in 1897 when the city's negotiators caved in and met Bute's demands.

The land, known then and now as Cathays Park, was to be used for several new civic buildings including a town hall, law courts, a museum and ultimately, a university. But there was serious opposition to the plan, led mostly by the city's daily newspaper, the Western Mail. Arguments about 'city-centre' shopping versus 'out-of-town' shopping centres go back a very long way indeed. It was precisely this issue that divided the supporters of the new civic centre from its opponents. The paper's editor, Lascelles Carr, was probably speaking for many of his merchant advertisers - all located in cluster in the middle of the town - when he wrote in one editorial of the "mysterious desire for removing the municipal buildings so far away from the centre of the town." Carr was talking about no more than seven or eight-hundred yards; the distance of the city's existing Town Hall from the proposed new site.

Built on a scale appropriate to the city's size, the Cathays Park Civic Centre is one of

Great Britain's finest manifestations of Victorian confidence and faith in the future. Its

imposing Portland stone buildings and their carvings celebrate the commerce, industry

and trade that made Britain the world's leading economy for much of the 19th century.

At a time of intense rivalry among the cities of the United Kingdom, Cardiff's city fathers

were determined that their community would stand comparison with any. What they

may not have known was that their extraordinary vision would also pave the way for the

city to make an international impact a century later.

Today the Park, and the meticulously manicured Alexandra Gardens, provide a stylish

setting for Cardiff University and its 15,000 students, the National Museum of Wales with

its world famous collection of Impressionist Art, as well as numerous government offices

such as the Welsh Office. Great Britain has a highly centralised government that until

recently was reluctant to share power with either local city councils or the three other

'nations' that make up the United Kingdom: Scotland, Northern Ireland and Wales.

"You're an American, right?" It is the most frequently asked question the Welsh put to 'Yanks.'

I was satisfying the curiosity of a well-dressed Welshman who had overheard me ordering a drink in a local pub. One query followed another until this genial local asked if I knew Chicago. After all, I was from the Midwest. I replied that I had some knowledge of this city of three million people that was 120 miles from my hometown.

"Did you ever run across someone by the name of Bob Smyth?"

"No, 'fraid not," I answered. "Chicago is a very big place and I only visited now and then with my dad to watch baseball."

There followed a poignant story from Clive Thompson, my new-found Welsh companion. As a boy, he had been raised in Bridgend, not quite a suburb of Cardiff but close enough to be so regarded by strangers. Like me, he had memories of the war. But his were far more vivid since he and his family had experienced the danger and deprivation, experiences civilians in American were spared.

In the huge logistical build-up for the Allied landings in France, the seaports of south Wales and the surrounding countryside were turned into a giant warehouse for men and munitions. Country lanes were lined with camouflaged tanks and trucks by the thousands. Supplies of food, gasoline, weapons and the whole array of war-making littered the landscape. Accompanying this vast armada were, of course, tens of thousands of G-Is. Mostly confined to encampments, some were given leave in nearby towns and villages. One was Bob Smyth, a U.S. Army sergeant from Chicago.

As a boy, Clive had already developed a certain entrepreneurial flare. And the chance to smuggle beer to thirsty soldiers where alcohol was strictly 'off limits' was an opportunity not to be missed. This is how he met Sergeant Smyth, trading him beer for chocolate, cigarettes, fruit and tinned goods - all luxuries that were severely rationed throughout the war in Britain. Indeed, much of the largesse Sergeant Smyth was able to 'appropriate' from the stacks of stores the American soldiers regarded as necessities, most people in Britain hadn't seen for years.

Once or twice during his brief stay in Wales, Smyth was granted liberty. As a way of showing their appreciation, the Thompson family invited him to Sunday lunch, a Welsh and British tradition. It must have been a rather Spartan affair since meat, eggs, butter and countless other varieties of food were rarely available. But the young sergeant from Chicago seemed to understand, and when he appeared at the Thompson home, he was laden with even more gifts for the family. Mrs Thompson saw her first nylons in five years. Mr Thompson was presented with a year's ration of tobacco in one lot. Bar after bar of precious chocolate 'candy' poured out of Smyth's tunic. The Thompson's were awe-struck.

Clive's trips to the U.S. base, his bicycle basket filled with bottles of beer that would be sneaked through the fence, were now a daily occurrence. Every afternoon, following school, he would make the short journey. Then one afternoon, he rounded the lane leading alongside the camp; got off his bike and peered through the fence. The tents that had housed thousands of soldier were gone. Sergeant Bob Smyth and his young comrades had gone to war.

Nearly a half-century later the kindness and generosity he had shown to a Welsh family had not been forgotten. And what had haunted Clive Thompson all those years was this question: did the young G-I survive the invasion, or was he one of the thousands who died liberating France and the continent from Nazi Germany? Clive and I made an effort to find out. Calls and letters to the Veterans Administration in Washington yielded nothing. Although helpful, they needed more than a name and a city.

I once asked him what he would say if we could locate Smyth. "I'd just like to say 'thanks'."

Today, walking through 'Cathays Park,' one could easily wonder why it created such a great fuss. Here is one of the world's most stunning collection of civic buildings, noteworthy for any number of reasons. First, it was built in a remarkably short period that must have been bursting with civic energy and enthusiasm. When it was at last opened to the public in May of 1899, the Park was a pleasant but very empty parcel of land. Within a mere fifteen years most of the buildings visitors admire today were either built or under construction. Moreover, those who drove this scheme forward were clearly inspired by a vision of what they wanted their city to become. Once the location had been secured, their unity of purpose was extraordinary.

Few cities owe so much to a single person. Throughout most of its history, the influence of the Bute family is evident. Thankfully, it was almost entirely a benevolent and positive influence.

The 3rd Marquess, whatever his personal quirks, had been an unrivalled benefactor to the city, and seems to have favoured the idea of a new and dazzling cluster of civic buildings for the community all along. He had

Totally out of proportion to their tiny numbers within Europe, the Welsh have had a very substantial impact on American history. Tens of thousands of Welsh immigrants brought their mining expertise to the coalfields of America. The ship that brought the Pilgrim Fathers to Plymouth, Massachusetts, the Mayflower, was captained by a Welsh seafarer. No less than seventeen of the 56 signers of the Declaration of Independence were of Welsh ancestry. Eleven Presidents could also claim to be of Welsh extraction, including Thomas Jefferson, Abraham Lincoln, and Richard Nixon. Yale University owes its existence to Elihu Yale, a native of Wrexham in North Wales where he is buried in the town's churchyard.

Two heroes of 'Dixie' in the American Civil War, Confederacy President Jefferson Davis, and the leader of the Southern armies, General Robert E. Lee, were both of Welsh background. In more modern times, the Welsh can count among their most prestigious 'exports' actors Richard Burton and Anthony Hopkins as well as the renowned architect, Frank Lloyd Wright, who named his Pennsylvania home after a famous Welsh poet of the Middle Ages, Taliesin.

even been elected mayor in 1891, and his flair for architecture and art was widely felt, from his ancestral home in Scotland to the building of one of the century's most unusual indulgences, the fairytale Castell Coch that overlooks Cardiff from the northern hills above the city.

"Everything that was good for Cardiff flowed from Bute," is the verdict of a modern architect. Stanley Cox teaches at Cardiff University's School of Architecture, itself located in the heart of Cathays Park. "Bute's image towers over it all," says Cox. "His investment in the port, Cathays Park, and now the regeneration of the docks. He would have applauded what is happening there today."

Like a ship's prow slicing through the waves

the bay

the bay

Like a ship's prow slicing through the waves

"Made fast at noon," reads the terse, business-like entry in the log of the Terra Nova for Friday, 10 June 1910. The ship had been waiting in Cardiff Roads in the Bristol Channel since the night before, and was now tied up in the Roath Dock at the berth of the Crown Patent Fuel Company, whose nearby offices were festooned with bunting and streamers to mark the occasion. On board was the Royal Navy officer who was to command the second 'National Antarctic Expedition,' Captain Robert Falcon Scott. A native of Devonport in the west of England, Scott had led the first historic 1901 expedition which had achieved a record latitude of 81° 17' south, the closest any explorer had come to the South Pole. In 1907, another attempt, this one led by British Army Major Ernest Shackleton, came even closer.

'Pole' fever, another manifestation of the great nineteenth century impetus for exploring every nook and cranny of the earth's surface, gripped the world. America's Admiral Peary had reached the North Pole in April of 1909, and come to Cardiff as part of his world lecture tour to talk about it. Norwegian Roald Amundsen, a veteran of years of Arctic exploration, was known to be keen to make an assault on the southern challenge. With Shackleton already holder of the 'furthest South' trophy, and aware of the rumours of French, Belgian, American and even Japanese proposals for expeditions, Scott was determined to be the first.

But it would take a very considerable sum of money. Scott insisted on emphasising the scientific nature of his venture, and of the party of 65 he planned to take, more than a fifth were researchers. The cost of so large an expedition was put at £50,000.

"Cardiff has led the way in helping us with our work of preparation," Scott told the Western Mail, and so it had. Within hours of the ship's arrival that June afternoon, the Crown Patent Fuel Company, in whose berth the Terra Nova now lay, began loading a gift of 300 tons of its unique fuel briquette, a mixture of compressed coal and bitumen that was much more efficient than coal alone, and would power the ship's steam engine when the winds for her sails failed. There were countless other gifts from the city, whose leaders had already raised £2,000 to help fund Scott's work. The Vacuum Oil Company provided engine and lamp oil. The Welsh Tin Plate Company presented the ship's company of sailors and scientists with pots and pans while other firms contributed everything from aneroid barometers to Stone's ginger wine. School children had collected enough donations to purchase tents, sleeping bags, dogs and ponies.

Behind this remarkable outpouring of support and generosity was the energetic editor of the Western Mail, W. E. Davies, who spared no effort, and devoted thousands of column inches, to publicise Scott's expedition and urge Cardiff's prosperous coal barons and businessmen to stand squarely behind it. Davies' contagious enthusiasm not only won over his readers, including the more affluent ones, but Scott as well. To show his gratitude, Scott promised to begin and end the voyage of the Terra Nova in Cardiff, establishing a unique relationship between himself, his venture and the hugely prosperous city.

The ship returned, but Scott did not. Scott and his comrades, including Welsh Petty Officer Edgar Evans, reached the South Pole on 18 January 1912, only to find the tent and flag of Amundsen who had achieved the goal five weeks earlier. The return journey ended in

the loss of the entire party, Scott dying of starvation and exposure on 29 March - a mere eleven miles from a supply depot.

Ironically and inexplicably, perhaps even inexcusably, visitors today will find little to commemorate 'Scott of the Antarctic' in the city that made his final expedition possible. To the cheers of vast crowds, surrounded by dozens of boats carrying hundreds more well-wishers, with the Cardiff flag flying at its fore and the Welsh flag on its mizen, the Terra Nova departed Cardiff that June to begin of one of the century's greatest adventures, an endeavour that in turn would become one of its most poignant tragedies. "I will reach the South Pole or I will never come back again," vowed Scott, little knowing how prophetic that pledge would become. He was 42 just days before the Terra Nova slipped its moorings in 'Tiger Bay,' and had only married two years before.

There is a 'Scott' Avenue in Cardiff, a nondescript monument in the city's Roath Park, and a plaque on the side of the once-elegant and bustling Royal Hotel where on the evening of 13 June 1910, Scott and the officers of the expedition were entertained at a gala dinner, guests of some of the most successful men in Britain at the time, men who had made incalculable fortunes from mining, selling and shipping coal, the treasure of the 'Black Klondyke.' But like Scott, their 'run of luck' was also about to end.

BRITISH SHIPS

Llanelly to Lord Erne

Name of Ship, and Port of Registry.	Signal Letters.
†Llanelly, Liverpool	P.G.F.M
†Llangibby, Cardiff	S.R.B.Q
†Llangollen, Cardiff	S.B.J.F
†Llangorse, Cardiff	R.N.H.T
†Llanishen, Cardiff	S.D.V.P
†Llanover, Cardiff	R.K.W.G
†Llansannor, Cardiff	R.Q.K.P
†Llanthony Abbey, Newport	M.B.H.Q
†Llanwern, Cardiff	H.G.K.S
†Llongwen, Cardiff	H.K.N.S
Loafer, Shoreham	H.M.L.F
Loango, Sligo	M.K.V.Q
†Lobelia, Hartlepool, W	M.V.J.L
Loch Broom, Glasgow	J.T.V.L
Loch Carron, Glasgow	J.V.R.C
Loch Etive, Glasgow	
Loch Finlas, Liverpool	
Loch Garry, Glasgow	
Loch Katrine, Glasgow	

Name of Ship, and Port of Registry.	
Lord Hamilton, Maldon	L.H.R.S
Lord Hartington, London	K.Q.B.F
†Lord Iddesleigh, London	K.T.D.G
†Lord Iveagh, Belfast	K.C.D.S
†Lord Kelvin, Liverpool	
†Lord Lansdowne, Belfast	
Lord Lansdowne, London	
†Lord Londonderry, Belfast	
†Lord Londonderry, Sunderland	
Lord March, Faversham	
Lord Napier, Glasgow	
†Lord Nelson, London	
Lord Nelson, Glasgow	

Roath Basin

Bute Docks. e

During its brief stay in Cardiff, Captain's Scott's Terra Nova would have been easily overlooked in a forest of masts that crowded the city's booming docks. The 1909 edition of Lloyd's Signal List of British Ships, the semaphore call signs by which commercial and military vessels were recognised throughout the world, counts nearly 2,000 cargo carriers in its columns. No less than 248 recorded Cardiff as their home port. Only much larger cities such as Glasgow, Liverpool, the Tyne River ship-building port of Newcastle, and Europe's largest commercial harbour, London, scored higher. By this time, most of the ships in Lloyd's list were driven by steam or a combination of steam and sail, a rapidly growing market for coal, especially the rich 'steam coal' that Wales produced in abundance.

By the early 20th century, Cardiff had become one of the world's busiest ports. Nearly forty countries had diplomatic representatives in the city, consul-generals who looked after their nations' and its citizens interests, be it a wayward sailor who had been jailed for drunkenness or a shipping contract. Behind the furious activity of the docks, and stretching almost to the city centre, lay Butetown and its grand Victorian offices and homes. One of the most impressive was the Coal Exchange. Here in a kind of miniature 'Wall Street Stock Exchange,' coal buyers and sellers met daily to noisily bargain, barter and deal while shipping agents hovered in the balconies overhead awaiting orders. Away from the hustle and the trading there was another side to Butetown, the notorious 'East Mud.' Here sailors from virtually every sea-going nation in the world could find what sailors ashore have always sought. Cardiff catered abundantly for their needs too,

providing services that made the port one of the roughest and toughest in the world.

But when the decline started it was rapid and economically disastrous. Just as the 19th century had seen a historic and massive inward migration of workers from across Europe, South Wales now began to experience a great exodus, and by 1950 it was estimated that a staggering 400,000 people abandoned forever the Rhondda and its neighbouring valleys. In the despairing words of Welsh writer Jan Morris: "So much struggle, so much fire, and nobody much richer in the end."

Incredibly, by the 1960s Cardiff was importing American coal. It was only the beginning. More would come from other countries as well, and on August 25, 1964, the Western Mail carried a story that was scarcely conceivable: "Cardiff ships its last load of coal." Up and down a roll-a-coaster ride that had taken a mere 125 years.

That the good burghers of Cardiff would keep their promise to help his expedition must have been evident to Captain Scott on his visits to the city. The dock area of the Welsh port was frenetic with activity in 1910, the zenith of coal production and exporting. For a half century, an army of miners had ranged over and under an area equivalent to 12 per cent of the entire land surface of Wales, in a veritable assault on the country's rich coal deposits, extracting millions of tons of the mineral that were transported to Cardiff and its sister port of Barry, a community created for the sole purpose of shipping coal to the world.

Early in the nineteenth century a canal had been driven from Merthyr in the Rhondda Valley down to Cardiff that required 50 locks in just over 25 miles, necessary since the canal head in the mountains behind the city was 568 feet higher than the sea lock on the Taff estuary. In one stretch, from Abercynon to Quaker's Yard, engineers built an incredible 16 locks in the space of a mile, locks that dropped barges 200 feet in the same distance. A single horse pulled each barge, the charge of a man and a boy helper. Although they were pathetically slow - covering only two miles in an hour - they were hugely efficient, carrying 24 tons of coal, a load that earlier had required no less than 12 horse-drawn wagons.

But even this heroic engineering effort was not enough. Hopelessly congested within months of its opening, the canal was unable to overcome another problem: it ended two miles from tidal low water in Cardiff, meaning that cargoes had to be loaded onto lighters and then off-loaded again onto sea-going ships. Such was the staggering and seemingly insatiable demand for coal that no expense was spared to get it to the ports, and the canal was augmented by the Taff Vale Railway in 1841. Meanwhile, in the bay on the doorstep of Cardiff, more docks were needed and were built, all funded from the deep pockets of the Marquesses of Bute.

Like the American heavy industry cities of Pittsburgh, Cleveland and Gary, and at about the same time, Cardiff flourished in a period of no environmental regulations, no health and safety laws, and minimal taxes.

Americans are by and large a thankful people, appreciating the unprecedented bounty their vast country has provided them over more than two centuries, the "amber waves of grain" and "purple mountain majesties above the fruited plain" that stretch from "sea to shining sea" that we celebrate in our unofficial anthem, America the Beautiful. We mark our gratitude for a real and symbolic harvest in a national holiday, Thanksgiving, an event no other nation observes. Just how bountiful, just how lucky and just how fortunate becomes starkly evident as I turn slowly through the pages of *Front Line: 1940 - 1941*, a cheaply-produced paperback published by the British "Ministry of Home Security" in 1942, and printed in the tens of thousands as part of the country's wartime propaganda effort.

Coming from a land virtually untouched by the

devastation of World War Two, Americans find it hard to visualise the terror, the horror, suffering and destruction that Britain experienced in the opening months and years of that conflict. *Front Line*, the government's "Official Story of the Civil Defence of Britain," makes you shake your head in incredulity: this really happened. By the summer of 1940, the German blitzkrieg had engulfed virtually all of continental Europe. France, Poland, Holland, Belgium and Denmark had all fallen, and across the 25 mile stretch we know as the English Channel, Hitler's armies were massing to take the last prize of his strategy, Britain itself.

It was a story closely followed by Picture Post, Britain's hugely popular weekly equivalent of America's Life magazine. It editor at the time, Tom Hopkinson, later to be knighted for a lifetime of service to British journalism, painted for me the grimmest of pictures of those far off days as he and I sat in his study in the Cardiff suburb of Penarth. "In 1940," he recalled, "when we were under threat of invasion, I knew, because I was on good terms with people in high positions, that our situation was literally desperate. If the Germans had landed in July, 1940, we hadn't got the tanks, even the rifles, nothing really to defend ourselves." It was Tom who generously gave me his only copy of *Front Line*, explaining that even though it was written and produced by government propagandists, it none the less was a truthful and accurate account of what Hitler had unleashed on Britain and its people. Indeed, many of the pictures the little book used had come from the pages of Picture Post.

The men and women who assembled those awful photos from the 'blitz,' the systematic bombing of nearly every major British city that went on for more than a year and was intended to be the Nazi's way of 'softening up' the island for the ultimate invasion, had heroic words and deeds to draw upon for their chronicle. For the publication, Winston Churchill himself wrote:

> I see the damage done by the enemy attacks; but I also see, side by side with the devastation and amid the ruins, quiet, confident, bright and smiling eyes, beaming with a consciousness of being associated with a cause far higher and wider than any human or personal issue. I see the spirit of an unconquerable people.

Both the Prime Minister and the Royal Family remained in London throughout the war, impatiently turning aside repeated pleas that they should be evacuated to safer surroundings. What they witnessed and shared with seven million Londoners, in night after night of

Luftwaffe raids, can only be imagined. The statistics, carefully compiled by the city's Fire Brigade and thousands of defence volunteers, are reeling. In the final three months of 1940, 12,696 civilians died from an estimated 36,000 bombs. Those who survived the awful blasts of high-explosive munitions were left to fight hundreds of simultaneously ignited fires from thousands of incendiary bombs. A staggering 700,000 homes were destroyed by blast and flames, with desperate fire-fighters standing knee-deep in the mud of the River Thames to pump water at low tide to replace the ruptured and useless water mains beneath the city's streets. Hitler had calculated that a 'knock-out' blow to the capital would bring Britain to its knees, but when it failed in the face of sheer and brazen British stubbornness and defiance, his airforce turned its attention to other cities.

His 1941 New Year's 'gift' to the people of Cardiff was a raid by 125 Luftwaffe bombers on the second night in January. That terrifying moment and more than two dozen additional raids that year left 299 dead in the Welsh capital. Most of the bombs were aimed and fell on Cardiff's docks, but one badly damaged the city's magnificent Llandaff Cathedral. But like its counterpart in London, the historic St Paul's, it remained steadfastly standing, and widely-distributed pictures of both became lasting and inspiring symbols of determination. In America, an issue of Life was devoted to the blitz of London, and the front cover carried one of the most striking photos to emerge from five years of war: the dome of St Paul's illuminated by the fires of countless buildings around it, but intact.

That first raid in Cardiff also produced a legend. That night, as the German planes turned to fly back to their bases, rescuers were led by the high-pitched singing of a child to the rubble of a Cardiff house. For hours they dug frantically through the remains of the home to the strains of "God Save the King." They eventually found a six-year-old boy huddled under what was left of a stairway. He told his rescuers his father had said to sing at the top of his voice if he became trapped, "because that's what the miners do in a cave-in."

docks that is now unfolding before them, and they are apt to name any of a dozen or more people. Looking across the expanse of the bay area from the vantage point of the Cardiff suburb of Penarth, and you begin to understand why there very well may be a scramble to say: "Oh, yes, I was the one who suggested this." Napoleon was right. Whoever takes credit, one thing is certain: a very considerable enterprise is underway here, one that seems destined to push Cardiff into the vanguard of the dynamic cities of the world, and one that is in its vision and impact is comparable to the building of Cathays Park more than a century ago.

"Victory," said Napoleon, "has a thousand fathers; defeat is an orphan." Ask political and civic leaders in Cardiff, local journalists or the 'man on the streets' to say who is responsible for the vast redevelopment of the city's

Scouring the records, newspaper accounts mostly, the first real mention I come across of a plan for regenerating 2,700 desolate acres of dockland, comes not from an imaginative politician, a civic leader or business executive - but from a relatively obscure

Truly the 'end of the line' in more

ways than one. Where once thousands

of coal cars rattled their way from the valleys

to the north, dumping their loads from the 'black

Klondyke' alongside the docks of Butetown, these steel

ribbons have not seen a train in decades, just as the massive

timber moorings yards away that once made fast the lines of

ships of the great oceans now rot. In the background of what stood

as landscape of despair stands another remnant of Cardiff's days as the

world's largest exporter of coal, the Pierhead building. Now a protected

monument that is being carefully incorporated and preserved in the new Bay

development, it was built in 1892 as the Cardiff Dock offices. Here hundreds of port and

railway officials kept coal for the furnaces, turbines, railway engines and steamships of their

customers flowing smoothly to destinations around the globe.

lecturer in town planning at what was then the University of Wales Institute of Science and Technology. The date is 1968, and the Western Mail, late in August of that year, carries a feature on its editorial page entitled "Butetown's role after Buchanan" by George Yeomans.

Today, George and his wife no longer live in Cardiff, but in a tiny hamlet in Pembrokeshire, the far west of Wales.

"Who," I ask him, "was Buchanan?"

"A town planner like myself," explains George.

It seems that Colin Buchanan, with a long career in the British civil service and the armed forces, had become an academic planner and a professor of transport at London's highly regarded Imperial College. Professor Buchanan's real interest was the car, and he had written a shelf-full of books and studies about the social impact of Henry Ford's vehicle for the common man. The

automobile was, in the Professor's view, a "mixed blessing," the name he gave to his widely read book published in 1958.

"In 1963," explained George, "Professor Buchanan was commissioned by the government to advise them on just what they could expect in the way of future problems the car would cause. The result was *Traffic in Towns*."

I found the Professor's study in the Cardiff University library. Reading through it, I began to understand why

his work was considered so important at the time. As in America and every other developed nation, but especially in the confined spaces of an island country such as Britain, the car was beginning to be seen as a truly 'mixed blessing.' In it he correctly predicts all of the congestion, delay and inconvenience we now associate with driving. The book earned Buchanan a knighthood, and triggered a national debate about the future of Britain's cities, one that went far beyond the impact of the car.

A specially shortened version of Buchanan's important report was published for one and all to read, and the introduction was written by one of Britain's most respected journalists, Sir Geoffrey Crowther, the long-serving editor of the prestigious Economist magazine. Crowther pulled no punches about the problems facing Britain's metropolitan areas: "Our cities, most of

them, are pretty depressing places, and to replan and rebuild them would be a worthwhile thing to do, even if we were not forced to it by the motor car."

That debate raged for years. Those cities like Portsmouth, Plymouth and Coventry that were truly obliterated by German bombing, had no choice but to rebuild. The question was how? In Cardiff, where Buchanan was commissioned by the city council to do a

drastic recommendations, such as demolishing 2,000 homes in the middle of the city to make way for, yes, highways and lots of them. The 'bulldozer' approach more common to American thinking about cities, had infected Buchanan.

second study devoted specifically to the Welsh capital, the damage inflicted by the Luftwaffe was minimal, but the decline of shipping and the effect it had on the city's dockland and its Butetown residents was pretty much the same: desolation and despair.

"Buchanan got a little carried away when it came to his plan for Cardiff," reckons George Yeomans. A kind of 'scientific' approach to town planning was popular at the time, he explains to me, "Number crunching, modelling, totally traffic-free zones, that sort of thing." Buchanan's plan for Cardiff included some rather

I asked architect Stanley Cox of Cardiff University's School of Architecture, who also remembered Buchanan's proposals, what he thought.

"Cardiff dithered, thank god," was his reply. "In addition to the idea about the houses that would have to go, Buchanan also wanted the city to build a ten-lane highway over the shopping area! It would be decked over with a kind of donut-hole left for the tower of St John's Church. Good sense thankfully prevailed and nothing was done. Meanwhile the debate went on and Cardiff remained one of the most underdeveloped cities in the United Kingdom in the post-war period."

It was precisely in the midst of this debate that George Yeoman's wrote his article for the Western Mail. Reading it today, thirty years later, I am struck by how accurately it foretells what would actually be done once the debates were exhausted, and civic momentum replaced talking. George Yeomans is far too modest to

claim credit for the direction the regeneration of the docks and Butetown itself took, but he could.

Read what he said three decades ago:

An in-town country park embracing East and West docks could include areas for walking, picnicking, sports pitches, fishing and watersports. Its empty dereliction is its strength, a rare opportunity for exciting proposals on a clean sheet, reaching from the centre to the sea…

Or,

Park, museum, Mount Stuart Square, National Theatre, all complimentary daytime attractions buttressing evening entertainment, enhancing the economy of shops, restaurants and public-houses, these in turn improving the appeal for offices and a place to live.

Buchanan took little interest in the docks and Butetown, and his plan for Cardiff, would in Yeoman's, view "reinforce Butetown's barriers, and assumes a rundown of its economy." He did not want to see the area written off as hopeless, a 'basket-case' beyond salvation.

Yeomans pressed on. While Cardiff, in the words of Stanley Cox, "dithered," Yeoman's carried on making

On the far edge of Cardiff Bay lies Penarth Marina. Its 230 pleasure boats have access to the broad Severn estuary and the Atlantic beyond through one of three locks in the Cardiff Bay Barrage, a dam that also gives yachtsmen a new playground on the Bay stretching right up into the city centre where until recently, tides exposed vast mudflats twice each day.

houses and taverns than the rest of the city combined, and a population that endured a rate of lethal tuberculosis seven times higher than the average for the city. Now the attitude is, he seemed to be saying, the money has been made, the last drop of blood, sweat and tears extracted from the docks, the captains and merchants coal and shipping helped make rich have departed, and we can forget about the area.

Was there a racial element in all this? Was Butetown neglected all of those years because of its long history of attracting West Indians, Africans of every country and tribe, and Asians from almost every nation? It is not difficult to make the case. This blend of races was there as it was in the neighbourhoods of virtually every seaport in the world, from New Orleans to Hamburg, Rotterdam to San Francisco and Brooklyn. Sailors do not always return home. Cardiff, like so many of the

the case for an imaginative, bold and visionary revival. But his concern went far beyond simply conservation of historic buildings and proposals for new and contemporary ways of using them. Unlike so many others who lived safely ensconced in a Cardiff suburb, far enough away to romanticise about the 'good ol' days' in Tiger Bay, Yeomans had no such illusions, pointing out that this was an area that once boasted more public world's great ports, now faced a dilemma: what does a city do with docklands when sea commerce is no longer important?

For different reasons, it was a situation most Americans, especially those from the larger US cities, would easily recognise. As they moved from the rural south to seek employment in the major urban areas, America's blacks were confined to the notorious 'inner cities.' For decades, white Americans took little notice of their abject poverty until the bloody race riots of the 1960s. There were occasional racial confrontations in Britain, including Cardiff, thankfully never on the scale of America's virtual wars in Los Angeles and Detroit and Cleveland. But the complacency and the prejudices of British whites would be depressingly familiar to any Afro-American.

Moreover, Cardiff was busy building its new commercial hub, St David's Centre, a stunning malled shopping district that complemented its historic arcades and featured the added attraction of one of Britain's leading concert halls. Butetown and its exotic racial mix, conveniently confined and enclosed by river and railway, was of little interest to anyone but its 6,000 residents - and a handful like George Yeomans. Years after putting forward his case in the Western Mail, he was doing the same in an academic journal, *Built*

Environment. Rehearsing the same arguments, and underlining again that to adopt Buchanan's proposals for Cardiff would only isolate Butetown even more, he concluded:

> The City Council seems suspicious that full-blooded revival here will prejudice investment in their city centre scheme. Their attitude is cool. Imaginative official action is imperative.

It was 1974, and George Yeomans and the few who thought like him, were about to get the action they sought.

"I lived down here. I worked down here. I made love down here. I sang down here."

I'm talking to a one-time plasterer who today sits in the House of Lords, the upper chamber of Britain's Parliament. He is Lord Brooks, 'Jack' to his many friends, and he would be immediately recognisable to any American. While he may have begun life as a working man, John Edward Brooks was later to become one very effective local politician, and would have been a smooth operator in the rough and tumble of American 'machine' politics, the kind that kept Chicago's long-time mayor, 'Boss' Daley in power for so long.

"You went wherever you could find a job in those days," continues Lord Jack, "and the only place I could find work was in the docks. I worked in every dock down here as a labourer, and after the war I spent my spare time down here too. The place stunk." He means that literally. When Cardiff's docks declined, so did neighbourhoods surrounding the old port, and the railway, the Great Western route from London and on through to the west of Wales, which neatly bisects the city, became a social divide as well.

"There were sixteen sewage outlets pouring into the Bay, and when the tide went out and left the mud flats showing, the whole place reeked, especially in the summer. Two-hundred yards away was a primary school, and people living down here, a lot of blacks. So, no one north of the tracks gave a damn."

But what about the 'good ol' days' of Butetown and 'Tiger Bay,' I ask.

"Rubbish! There weren't any 'good ol' days.' The incidence of TB down here was the highest in the country. Those who talk about how wonderful it was, just don't know. I don't remember anything good about the past."

His father was a plasterer, and so was his grandfather, who helped build the stunning civic centre in Cathays Park a century before. A member of the Labour Party for more than fifty years, Jack Brooks quickly became involved in local politics, first in one of the country's most powerful unions, the Transport and General Workers, and then in the County Council. He rose to the top, for two years chairman of the Labour Party in Wales. For 20 years he was probably the most powerful politician in Cardiff, one of the most influential in the country, and when the Labour Party took over both the city and county government in 1974, Lord Brooks was elected leader of what was then the Glamorgan County Council.

"In the 80s, I came down here to Butetown and I was appalled. I went back to the Council and said, 'something's got to be done, the place is a disaster.' " And what Lord Brooks determined to do arguably triggered one of the most imaginative urban redevelopments in all of Europe. Today, the 'pagoda-like' headquarters of local government in Cardiff, where the city and county bureaucracy has been combined into what Americans know as 'Unigov,' is in Cardiff Bay. It was almost single-handedly his creation. But persuading his fellow councillors to re-locate the County's offices and its hundreds of employees was an uphill struggle.

The home of local government in the Welsh capital, Cardiff County Hall was the first

significant building to be located in the Bay. That reaffirmation of the area's future triggered

the Bay development that is now pushing across the vast re-claimed docklands, an area equal

to one-sixth of the whole city. Even Prince Charles, noted for his scathing comments on

contemporary British architecture, was pleased with the imaginative pagoda-like structure.

"I used to take the view that if I was going to do something, do it big. I don't listen to sceptics. We needed a new building, and I wanted it in the Bay. But I also knew I needed support, so I went to Geoff Rich." If there was another man as powerful in Cardiff as Lord Jack, it was the editor of the city's local paper, Geoff Rich of The Echo.

"We went a long way back, Geoff and me. Our fathers knew each other. I said, 'Geoff, this is about more than a building; it's about opening up the land down here.' He said he'd back me." And back him The Echo did, with priceless publicity and support. The imposing Cardiff County Hall is truly 'the house that Jack built.' More importantly, it was the beginning of a turnaround.

By the time County Hall was finished and opened in the autumn of 1988, Lord Brooks and his Labour Party allies in South Wales were operating in a less friendly environment than when he first entered politics 15 years earlier. For Americans, used to a political system where the White House and Washington have little effect and even less power over local government, it is at first hard to appreciate just how much the towns, cities and counties of Great Britain are dominated by the occupant of 10 Downing Street, the residence of the Prime Minister. The United Kingdom's highly centralised government bears little resemblance to the many independent tiers of American government. While national laws apply at the state, county and local level, the federal system of the United States simply doesn't allow for a President to have the power over a state legislature, a governor or a mayor that is found in Britain. Here also, to be a Conservative or Labour member of Parliament means being subject to rigorous control of the party 'whips' who can do incalculable

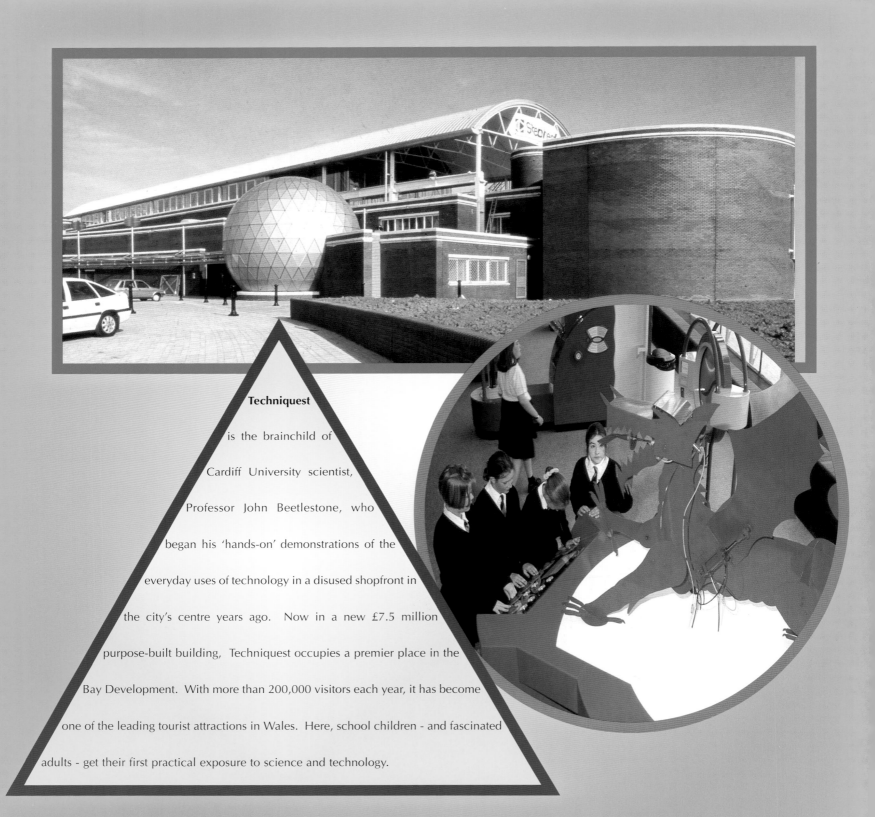

Techniquest

is the brainchild of

Cardiff University scientist,

Professor John Beetlestone, who

began his 'hands-on' demonstrations of the

everyday uses of technology in a disused shopfront in

the city's centre years ago. Now in a new £7.5 million

purpose-built building, Techniquest occupies a premier place in the

Bay Development. With more than 200,000 visitors each year, it has become

one of the leading tourist attractions in Wales. Here, school children - and fascinated

adults - get their first practical exposure to science and technology.

Like a ship's prow slicing through the waves, the sharp-edged NCM building faces squarely to the sea. Here, 400 employees of The Netherlands company enjoy a working environment one of them compares to "a five-star hotel." Wales' leading newspaper, The Western Mail, called the building "probably the finest structure to be completed in Wales since Cathays Park." The ambitious Bay development is the third major improvement for the Welsh capital that began in the late nineteenth century with Cathays Park, the civic centre, then moved to a wholesale redevelopment of its shopping area with the expansive St David's Centre, and is now complete with a regeneration of 2,700 acres of derelict docklands in the Bay. Together, they virtually catapult Cardiff into a 'world-class' city.

damage to a political career if an ambitious politician doesn't 'toe the party line.' Americans are often asked what it means to be a 'Democrat' or a 'Republican.' The answer is: 'Not much.'

There are some parallels, however, and Wales provides one of them . Since the end of the American Civil War more than 100 years ago, the South - until recent times anyway - was the bedrock of the Democratic Party. Any US politician who aspired to the Presidency could count on the support of virtually every voter and politician south of the 'Mason-Dixon Line.' Similarly here, there is little a Conservative Prime Minister can depend on in the way of support from Wales, which has always been and still remains solidly Labour. And since the cities and towns of Britain have little power, especially when it comes to budgets and money, virtually every initiative beyond raising taxes to pay for filling chuckholes in the street to collecting garbage has to be approved by London, starting first with the consent of London's 'governor-general' of the Principality, the august Secretary of State for Wales. Scotland and Northern Ireland have the same powerful potentate, all appointed by the party in power in London. Some Secretaries of State have had little or no real connection to the 'nation' they govern, elected Conservatives being particularly scarce in Wales and Scotland. Through all of Mrs Thatcher's long reign, the posts were held by Conservatives, creating in Wales and even more so in Scotland, tension not far from the unease that must have existed between Rome's Pontius Pilate and the conquered people of Palestine. Imagine a Republican President of the United States making one of his closest political 'pals' the Governor of an American state dominated by Democrats, and you get the picture.

Clearly any idea for the regeneration of Cardiff Bay had more than a few hurdles to leap before it could become a reality.

Days later and I'm with another Lord, but an entirely different member of the species *humanus politicus*. Tall, well-spoken and elegant, Nicholas Edwards shares only one quality with Lord Brooks: both are Welsh. He lists fishing, gardening, collecting water-colours and drawings as his hobbies. Jack Brooks is a boxing enthusiast. Nicholas Edwards, now Lord Crickhowell, is a graduate of Britain's elite Cambridge University. In America he would have gone to Harvard or Yale. Jack Brooks remembers singing in a Tiger Bay bar with Cardiff-born Shirley Bassey when she was a teenager, and long before she became an international star. It is hard to imagine Nicholas Edwards singing with anyone. The comparisons could go on, but all make the same point: these two men have virtually nothing in common except their 'Welshness' and love of politics, and even there, predictably one is Labour, the other Conservative. About as far apart as say, Ronald Reagan was from President John F Kennedy.

"If you're going to attract inward investment," Lord Crickhowell is saying to me over his lunch in the 'Celebrity Restaurant' of Cardiff's splendid concert auditorium, St David's Hall, "then be sure and build some golf courses."

That remark, often repeated by his political enemies as typical of an upper-class Tory, is rather more sensible than it first may seem. As the Secretary of State of Wales, the ultimate representative of London's authority in one of the four 'nations' that make up the United Kingdom, repairing the damage of decades of

A dark blue cross outlined in white on a bright red field, the flag of Norway flies on a staff next to the Norwegian Church in Cardiff Bay. It was originally built as one of dozens of seaport missions around the world to provide spiritual guidance to Norwegian sailors who otherwise might stray from the strict regimen of the Evangelical Lutheran religion, the national church in a country where nearly one-hundred per cent of the population are members, including the King. Their Scandinavian forefathers were not as restrained. As the notorious 'Vikings' they invaded much of Britain's coastline hundreds of years ago including Wales, where some trace of their past can be found to this day in the names of islands along the Welsh coast such as 'Steepholm' and 'Flatholm.'

The old church, which had ministered to sailors for decades, was delicately dis-assembled piece-by-piece by a trust, formed by enthusiasts, and stored until it could be re-assembled on a new site. Today, overlooking the sea that brought sailors to its simple portals, it is a popular coffee shop and restaurant, and only the occasional venue for a religious service.

For Norwegians, ports like Cardiff are still warmly associated with their history. Not long ago, I met a young Norwegian couple making their way to the city on a train from London. Asked the reason for their visit, I was told they wanted to get married in the Welsh capital. Why? The groom explained: "It's where my father, a sea captain, married my mother, a cook on another Norwegian ship."

Today, Norwegian visitors to Cardiff are often jokingly told: "I hope you not here to pillage and burn and carry off our women like Eric the Red."

decline in Wales was very much his responsibility. When you now see the number of Japanese, American and German businessmen playing golf on one of the many courses that now dot the landscape of South Wales on a Saturday morning, taking a break from their jobs of running the many factories that now dot the South Wales landscape, you also see the wisdom of his thinking. Just as Lord Brooks saw the utter necessity of turning around a half-century of industrial and shipping collapse in 'Tiger Bay,' Lord Crickhowell recognised the compelling urgency to regenerate the whole of the devastated South Wales economy. As it turned out, their twin visions were not unrelated.

"When you are Secretary of State for Wales, you are the minister for all of the domestic field of government with a real ability to do things," he tells me. "I was lucky because I was there long enough, longer than most ministers in their cabinet jobs, to see things through, seven or eight years."

He was helped in as much as that period marked the pinnacle of power for one of the longest-serving and most remarkable politicians in all of Britain's lengthy history: Margaret Thatcher. It was she who appointed the then Nicholas Edwards as Secretary of State for Wales, but he was constantly aware that however supportive of his ideas in his new post, she and most of her administration were still English.

"The rest of Britain is curiously ignorant about anything that happens in Wales," he offers. "It has been much easier to sell Wales to the Japanese or the American inward investor. I sometimes found, funnily enough, more knowledge about Wales on the other side of the world than there is in England. Very few people in

England have any idea about Cardiff, and when you tell them it has one of the most beautiful and impressive urban centres of any capital city in any country, they are all pretty sceptical."

When in 1979 he took office in the massive Welsh Office overlooking Cathays Park, the seat of Her Majesty's Government in the Principality, proposals for assisting this or that declining valley or community in Wales were stacked deep on his desk. He tackled the job with vigour, and few today dispute the success he made of it. The roster of foreign companies he persuaded to set up in Wales reads like the Fortune 500 list of international firms. It took a while, but eventually he came to the folder marked: 'Cardiff docks.' And on a typically cold, wet and windy winter morning in 1985, he and one of his aides decided to see for themselves what a programme of regeneration of the Bay might mean.

"We stood there thinking this was once the greatest coal port in the world. But now, here in the heart of Cardiff, the Welsh capital, was a vast tract of derelict and wasted land. It was gloomy beyond words. Cardiff, separated from its docks was like a ship with a

missing mast. Most of the posh people in the city hadn't ventured down there in years. We didn't take long to conclude that something had to be done."

Jack Brooks, who had reached the same conclusion, now had an unlikely ally.

Throughout the Bay, art links Cardiff with its past as a leading seaport. Promenades, walkways, plazas and terraces have been chosen for spotting innovative but functional art over the entire area, most of it reminding visitors that the Bay was once a gateway to the world's oceans. Including art in its brief to contractors from the earliest days, the Bay Development Corporation set up the Cardiff Bay Arts Trust and helped fund commissions for work from world-class sculptors and many Welsh artists as well.

"This is what men have built, and is not everything then possible?" The words of the Welsh-born scholar Raymond Williams, whose thinking about the 'cities of man' influenced an entire generation. He wasn't talking about Cardiff, but he could have been. These sprawling, teeming clusters of people that we call cities come in a hundred varieties. Some are more than pleasant; they are a joy to behold and call 'home.' Others we want to put behind us as quickly as we came upon them.

Neither Jack Brooks nor Nicholas Edwards would regard themselves as 'visionaries.' But talk to them long enough, and the language of men who dream begins to surface. When you get to know them, this kind of musing is typical of politicians. After all, what is power if it cannot be used to make dreams a reality, to leave a lasting mark? I sense however, that it took them a while to discover they were really chasing the same rainbow, and that only together could they do something about their shared ambition for Wales and its capital. Both went about realising the dream in their own style.

Lord Crickhowell returned to his elegant offices in Cathays Park that rainy morning and ordered his civil servants to come up with a plan. Weeks later, one of them, Freddie Watson, came back with an idea: 'We will build a barrage.' It was rather extreme in more than one sense. The proposal was to dam the entire estuary of the River Taff where it joins the Severn. In engineering terms it would be a considerable challenge, but that was as nothing compared to the political feat of getting it funded.

"We knew it could be done," Lord Crickhowell told me, "and we went off to Baltimore to see what it might look like."

Like Cardiff, the seaport of Baltimore after World War II faced what appeared to be terminal decline, and then the idea of creating its now-famous 'Inner Harbour' was proposed.

"Baltimore was interesting to us because its old dock area is almost exactly the same size as Cardiff's. In a remarkably short period of time, Baltimore had managed to create the Inner Harbour, swanky hotels and restaurants, and linked the old city with its seafront. It was all happening there and it was a great success. Yes, Baltimore became our inspiration."

In late 1986, Secretary of State for Wales Nicholas Edwards was ready to go public with the idea: build a barrage between suburban Penarth on the west side of Cardiff Bay to the entrance of one of the old docks on the other, creating a lake which would cover the tidal mud flats and extend up the Taff River right into the city centre. Around it was nearly 3,000 acres of land immediately available for development or refurbishment, with 600 acres on the water's edge. This was a vision indeed.

"There was great enthusiasm for the project, but I knew from talking to those who were so successful in Baltimore that it would need firm and consistent control," he explained in launching the idea. "We will above all need a clear plan, careful zoning and the protection of key sites, especially a waterside walk."

"Firm and consistent control" was Lord Crickhowell's way of assuring his political superiors in the Thatcher government and his political opponents in Cardiff that this project would not be turned over to Cardiff's political leaders entirely, but that they would be 'consulted.' What Mrs Thatcher did not want was another London Docklands, a project to redevelop the docks of Europe's largest city that had been largely destroyed by German bombing. That vast enterprise nearly ended in disaster, politically and in every other sense, largely because it was imposed on local people and was implemented without an overall plan.

Speaking with a familiarity that presumably only a handful could use about the imperious Prime Minister, Lord Crickhowell says "I knew I had to persuade Margaret and the Treasury, who get very nervous when a Minister starts talking about spending millions. In the end, I effectively had to threaten resigning, or implying I would, knowing how that would go down six months ahead of a General Election."

With a skill that even Jack Brooks would admire, Lord Crickhowell then convinced the Prime Minister to visit Cardiff, and see for herself what he had in mind. "I took her up to the top of a building in the Bay and we made a few photographs of her with what I hoped was an approving gaze." Geoff Rich's Echo carried the pictures on its front page.

"You can't warm to Nick Edwards, you know," says Lord Brooks, "He's a bit of a cold fish." South Glamorgan County Council Leader Jack Brooks had been summoned to London, to meet the Secretary of State and hear of his plan. They sat, surrounded by the Minister's civil servants in the stately splendour of

Gwydyr House in Whitehall, the London home of the Welsh Office.

"He sat back in his chair, stared at the ceiling and went off to enjoy a soliloquy. 'I don't like the sound of this,' I said to myself. I interrupted him, and you're not supposed to do that, you know. 'Secretary of State,' I said, 'if you are leading me to accept a London Docklands type of set-up in Cardiff, sorry but you'll get no co-operation from me.' His face went as black as thunder and he stood up and said: 'Very well, let me have your thoughts on paper.' I told him he would have them in two days."

Council Leader Brooks demanded two things: no powers must be taken from any local authority and the local political leaders must be represented on any board set up. He got both, and the way was now clear create

the Cardiff Bay Development Corporation, a 'quango' - acronym for 'quasi-autonomous-non-governmental-organisation.' This strange creation, a blend of leaders from every organisation, public and private with an interest in the Bay's development, would steer the project through to completion. He made Sir Geoffrey Inkin its chairman, a Conservative much admired for his leadership qualities by Lord Crickhowell and many others. The deputy chairman would be none other than Jack Brooks, what Lord Crickhowell calls 'a conscious decision.'

CARDIFF BAY

Europe's most exciting waterfront

When Lord Crickhowell - then Nicholas Edwards, the Welsh Secretary - sought ideas for the development of Cardiff's dockland, he and his aides quickly hit upon Baltimore, Maryland. Like the Welsh capital, this American eastern seaboard city had depended for decades on the commerce of the sea, and when that trade declined, so did Baltimore's waterfront.

Today, its Inner Harbour, finished in 1980, attracts five million visitors a year. Unlike Cardiff, the renaissance of Baltimore was driven forward by businessmen, notably the remarkable American developer, James W Rouse. In an issue that featured him on the cover, Time magazine called him 'the world's leading urban evangelist,' and it was his relentless dynamism that gave America its first shopping malls, affordable urban housing for the poor, and the beginning of Baltimore's extraordinary revival. Rouse knew of poverty first hand. When his father died, leaving the family with staggering business debts, the banks stepped in and foreclosed on the family home. Forced to drop out of the University of Virginia at the height of the Great Depression, Rouse began a career in development in his home state of Maryland. When he died in 1996 at the age of 81, the Rouse Company was valued at $450 million. In 1995, President Clinton awarded him America's highest civilian honour, the Freedom Medal. At the ceremony in the White House, Rouse remarked: "You can do something good in this world or you can make money. The trick is to make money while doing good; that's real success."

Baltimore was founded in 1706, a port on the banks of the huge Chesapeake Bay that first handled the produce of local farmers. It was a thriving centre of sea commerce long before Cardiff, and today is a much larger city than the Welsh capital with a population of nearly two and one-half million. Its famous sons and daughters include Billie Holiday, F. Scott Fitzgerald, 'Mama' Cass Elliot and the Duchess of Windsor, Wallis Simpson.

Baltimore was the birthplace of that centre-piece of American patriotism, the Star Spangled Banner. Although the thirteen colonies had won their independence from Great Britain in the revolution of 1776, America was at war again with the mother country in 1812-14. After capturing Washington and burning the White House, the British forces turned to their second objective, the key port of Baltimore. But their fleet was turned back at Fort McHenry, the engagement that ended the conflict. Watching the siege of the fortress on the night of September 13, 1814, was the 35-year-old lawyer and poet, Francis Scott Key. Ironically, Key wrote the poem to match the meter of an English hymn. It was only in 1931 that Congress made the lyrics and music America's national anthem.

> Oh, say can you see, by the dawn's early light,
> What so proudly we hailed at the twilight's last gleaming?
> Whose broad stripes and bright stars, through the perilous fight,
> O'er the ramparts we watched, were so gallantly streaming?
> And the rockets' red glare, the bombs bursting in air,
> Gave proof through the night that our flag was still there.
> O say, does that star-spangled banner yet wave
> O'er the land of the free and the home of the brave?

As the project unfolded, both would play their appropriate roles on their respective sides of a winding and sometimes tricky path, but one that led to the same destination. In Parliament, the Minister of State had to successfully steer through a bill authorising the barrage. In the end, it would take six years. In the Council Chambers, Leader Jack Brooks faced no less than 21 'anti-barrage' resolutions. In the House of Lords, Lord Crickhowell would ally himself with another Labour Lord, the former Prime Minister James Callaghan who - as luck would have it - had represented a Cardiff constituency including the bay area, and liked the idea of the barrage and the entire Bay development project. In Cardiff, Jack Brooks had to rely on a kind of politics that would have been familiar to 'Boss' Daley in Chicago, and countless other 'wheeling and dealing' American politicians.

"One night," he tells me, "I was fed up with anti-barrage resolutions and we had a meeting of the party with another one of these on the agenda. I looked around the meeting and I was out-numbered.

"Democracy, don't forget, is about numbers, about arithmetic. This chap got up to move the resolution and I thought: 'What am I going to do?' I looked up and saw I was under the smoke alarm. Now, no smoking is allowed in the meetings, but I lit my pipe, said 'Oh, sorry,' and blew the smoke straight up into the alarm. The bloody thing was making a hell of a racket all over the building. The porter rushed in and said: 'Everybody out!' Two fire engines arrived. I knew the young fireman in charge and he looked at me and asked, 'What

room are you in?" I said never mind about that, how long will it take you to search this building from top to bottom? 'That's a two hour job,' he said. I told him: 'You start at the top and work your way down.' We all had to go home."

How can two men, who in any other context would find themselves on opposite sides, become allied to the same cause? Americans call it common-sense, although we probably inherited this useful political skill from the British. Their history is replete with such examples. It is largely why a relatively small nation was able to acquire and maintain an empire that spanned the globe for more than a century, and why today they remain, though much weakened, a formidable voice and influence in affairs everywhere. In Britain it is called 'pragmatism,' and Nicholas Edwards and Jack Brooks are both sublime examples of practical men. Lord

Crickhowell attributes it to the smallness of Wales where everyone shares the same objectives.

Today, a decade into their project, both Lord Brooks, now in his seventies, and Lord Crickhowell, who just turned 65, are pensive and reflective about what both could rightly regard as a crowning achievement in long political careers.

"Every time I come down here, yes, I do get a bit of a tingle," says Lord Crickhowell. "I can't help but think of that rainy day so many years ago and the awful impression I came away with. We've changed it. It is different and that's exciting."

Jack Brooks stares thoughtfully out the window of his office in the Cardiff Bay Development Corporation's headquarters and lights his pipe. Smoking is allowed and thankfully there is no alarm overhead. For several minutes he says nothing, and then: "Jim Callaghan once said to me: 'Jack, you know, we'll all be forgotten when this is over.' I said, 'Jim, Prime Ministers are never forgotten; leaders of local councils are.'

"Look around this city today," he says. "You're from the outside. Tell me, is there anything we don't have? Cardiff is almost a city-state. When I look back, when I was 20 years old, working down here - well, who would think that I would be talking this way some day."

The good ship Cardiff now had all its masts.

Alan Davies is a former British army officer who used to stage war games in the Cardiff docks. Born in Cardiff, Davies is a graduate of Sandhurst, the British equivalent of America's West Point. These days, he is back in his hometown, but his assignment could not be more different: property development in the renewed Cardiff Bay as the executive director of a company called Grosvenor Waterside.

"When the Cold War was still underway," he tells me, "I was here with the army to practice securing the port of Cardiff. In the event of a 'hot' war, we knew that Cardiff would be an important link in the supply chain of munitions, and we had detailed plans to hold it, and occasionally we tried out our plans."

Then the docks, instead of swarming with sailors and stevedores as it had during the coal boom, was virtually

empty. "It was a mess; it was dying." Today, his elegant office overlooking the Bay development, is in the century-old Pierhead Building, the same structure where an uncle worked in the 1920s. From thriving port, the largest exporter of coal in the world, to bleakness - all in the space of a mere two generations of the Davies' family. His uncle would be overwhelmed by what is happening today in the docks, and no doubt more than a little pleased that his 51 year old nephew is at the centre of a remarkable reversal of what must have seemed a hopeless downward spiral.

"To understand what I am doing, and the role of Grosvenor Waterside," Davies explains, "you have to go back to early 80s when the Thatcher government privatised what was then the

British Transport Docks Board." With a faith in market forces and capitalism that would rival any of America's most zealous champions of free enterprise, and bent on reversing what she saw as Britain's decline as an industrial power, Mrs Thatcher began selling off one public enterprise after another: ports, airlines, the railways, the coal and steel industry, the entire telephone system, and in one case, even an automobile company - in short, any government agency she thought would be better and more efficiently operated by business. Most were floated on the London Stock Exchange, and brought in billions of pounds of revenue to Her Majesty's Treasury. More importantly however, it meant that civil servants and bureaucrats were replaced by businessmen and entrepreneurs, and that the 'market place,' not politicians, would make the decisions. Tolerating no opposition, she roared through a list of public companies at breakneck speed and

insisted all be sold, upending decades of socialism under successive Labour governments. It was an extraordinary act of faith in capitalism, and by and large has worked. Even the country's present Labour administration, far more politically centrist than its predecessors, has no plans to take any of these enterprises back into public ownership.

When it came to the harbours scattered along Britain's long coastline, docks that like Cardiff had declined alarmingly, one of the buyers was Associated British Ports. The 'package' they bought included the Cardiff docks, along with more than 20 other ports. Realising that the vast tracks of land they now owned could also be used for profitable property development, they set up a subsidiary to do precisely that.

"Grosvenor Waterside is the property developer of

ABP here in Cardiff," Davies explains. "Since 1991 - after the Cardiff Bay Development Corporation provided the infrastructure of roads, sewage and communications - we have had the task of encouraging private property development, mostly offices and residential buildings." As luck would have it, the heart of the Bay development is focused on land owned by ABP and developed by Grosvenor Waterside, 140 choice acres at the water's edge.

"Since 1992, we have spent £63 million on what you see around you today. Of that, £6 million came from the

government, meaning a 'leverage' of ten-to-one."

'Leverage' is the financial world's jargon for turning a few pounds or dollars into many, many more. "It means," says Davies, "that with everything else Cardiff has going for it, the city can 'punch above its weight' not just in Britain, but the world. What is happening here is so close to the city's centre that we really are part of Cardiff where two million people live within a commuting time of an hour."

By any measure, Davies and his colleagues have been successful. They have persuaded company after company to locate in the Bay.

"Take Atlantic Wharf as an example," he says. "This development of a 12-screen cinema, restaurants, a 24-lane bowling alley and parking for a thousand cars was sold for £30 million to British Airways' pension fund

before the foundations were complete. They knew, as we did, that it would be a success." No one can argue with that. Now finished, the complex attracts huge crowds that a few years ago would never have thought of coming to 'Tiger Bay.' The parking lot is frequently overflowing.

Similarly with NCM, the insurance giant. When the company began looking for a new headquarters in the UK, Cardiff Bay was chosen. But then came a very challenging brief to the architects: all 400 employees were to effectively have a 'window seat,' and there were to be no barriers separating one work area from another. As I walked through the building one summer morning speaking to one NCM staffer after another, it was hard to believe we were in a building since most of the 'walls' are glass and command a panoramic vista over the Bay. "It's like

being outside all year," one told me, "but without getting wet."

Days later, I was to get very wet when Alan Davies turned me over to a colleague, Cardiff Port Administrative Manager, Barry Angulatta. He showed me what the public do not see, and even when the Bay development is finished, still will not see: the working port. For a very long time, those of us who paid any attention have been given the impression that shipping is one of the world's 'sick' industries. The impression is wrong. True, fewer ships ply the oceans, crewed by only a fraction of the sailors previously needed, but they are larger and faster, and carry cargoes to and from Cardiff that range from frozen orange juice, steel, grain and - hard to believe - coal. The city which once supplied coal

to the world, now imports it, largely from Poland, South Africa and America.

Barry has seen it all in 38 years working in the port. When he began, the Cardiff docks were privately owned. After the war the Labour government took them into public ownership, and then in 1981, back

Unlike many American cities, where entire communities have been bulldozed to provide freeways for city centre workers fleeing to the suburbs, Europeans refuse to make the same sacrifice on the altar of the automobile. Rather than destroy a whole neighbourhood in Cardiff's old docklands with a four-lane swath of concrete, the Bay Corporation elected instead to tunnel under it for more than half a mile at very considerable expense.

The tunnel is part of a £135 million 'peripheral distributor road' that links the Bay development area to the nearest motorway, the M-4.

they went into commercial hands. Rather surprisingly perhaps, he is very upbeat about the future of Cardiff as a port. We are standing alongside the Queen Alexandra lock. Longer than three football fields and nearly as wide, it was built more than one hundred years ago. "A dozen ships would lock through in those days," Barry explains. "Today, we can handle only one in the same space; that's how big they have become."

He makes a point about shipping that occurs to few: the environment. "As the pressure increases on road transport, and as trade expands within the European Community, ports like Cardiff can only grow." Already more than 1,200 ships call at the port each year, and it is increasing.

Without question the most unusual caller is the St Helena, a mailship that is the only link with the tiny dot of the same name in the South Atlantic which was the home of the exiled Napoleon. Today, without an airport, the island colony relies on the four trips a year the ship makes from Cardiff. "Since satellite television came in a few years ago," says Barry, "it carries a lot of TV sets and videos." The St Helena also carries up to 90 passengers, and is popular with tourists seeking an unusual holiday since she also stops at Tenerife and Ascension islands as well as Cape Town.

Over the massive lock gates, Barry and I peer down 38 feet to the sea below. In a few hours the tide will rise by the same amount, and the lock gates will have to be opened. "If we didn't open them, the pressure of the tide would force them open and damage the machinery."

On our way back to his office, also in the historic Pierhead Building, we pass a large modern freighter where brighly coloured barrels are being unloaded. "Frozen orange juice from Brazil," Barry tells me. "It's concentrated and will be stored in that cold store alongside the ship at minus 28 degrees Celsius until water is added and it is bottled for supermarkets all over this area."

What's the most unusual cargo you've handled? I ask him. "Baby Cham, an entire shipload of it, little bottles of sparkling wine, all going to France." Rather like bringing coal to Cardiff when you think about it.

Costing more than £198 million, the Cardiff Bay Barrage snakes its way across the mouth of two rivers. More than 20,000 tons of steel sheet piling, 140,000 tons of concrete, and 1.5 million cubic yards of rock and sandfill went into a structure that really has only one purpose: to halt the daily tidal flows and create a lake with an eight-mile long waterfront. But its construction involved more than brute engineering. Architects and landscape designers had an equal role to play in what is really one of the largest cosmetic exercises in recent civil engineering history, what one of them calls 'Covent Garden by the sea.'

Balfour Beatty and Costain. Names you and I have seen on signs around the world, especially where massive civil engineering works are underway, companies whose construction skills are manifest from dry docks in Dubai, the massive flood barrier across the River Thames, the new Chek Lap Kok Airport in Hong Kong, the Pergua hydro-electric dam in Malaysia, a new library in Egypt, and even earthquake reinforcement on San Francisco's Golden Gate Bridge.

When it came to building this barrier, a dam across the two main rivers of South Wales that will create a 'tide-less' lake of 500 acres and a permanent waterfront more than seven miles long, the Cardiff Bay Development Corporation turned to these two international giants of civil engineering.

One rainy morning, I am standing in a very big hole in the ground, a hole with a difference: it is normally under water, and lots of it. Balfour Beatty and Costain engineers have dug 20 feet into the seabed, surrounded a vast excavation with a protective temporary 'coffer' dam bigger than the finished barrage itself, and are now completing work on three enormous locks that will allow pleasure boats access in and out of the lake that will soon cover the once heavily polluted tidal mudflats that provided Butetown with its own special aroma.

My engineer-guide, whose own experience with Balfour Beatty has taken him to far-flung corners of the world, explains that outside the coffer dam, the sea is at maximum high tide. "It means that on the other side of that wall of rock, stone and sand, there's another 40 feet of water above us," he explains. A quick bit of mental arithmetic tells me that were it not for barrier around us, we would be under 60 feet of Atlantic tide pushing up the Severn estuary.

Hundreds of men are at work. Through the rain I can see pumps, cranes, generators, compressors, and dump trucks large enough to carry a good-sized house. Inexplicably, it is strangely quiet in the midst of one of the largest civil engineering projects currently underway in Europe. I soon find out why. When these two companies formed the consortium that won them the contract to build the barrage, they also took on an

unprecedented obligation detailed in the 'small print,' one that made history in the world of civil engineering: to keep the noise, disruption, upheaval and inconvenience to thousands of local residents to an absolute minimum.

"We are required," explains my guide, "under the penalty of severe fines, to not exceed 75 decibels of sound any time from seven in the morning until seven in the evening." That's about as loud as normal conversation from the person sitting next to you. Moreover, just to make sure they are within the limits, three monitoring stations, linked to a computer and costing £20,000 each, are strategically spotted around the site. The companies developed a 'computer noise model' that instantly tells them if the sound nearby residents heard was the construction, a 747 about to land at Cardiff International Airport, or - as in several cases - seagulls that sat squawking as they perched on the system's sensitive microphones. Each sound, man-made or natural, creates its own unique 'noise signature.'

"Every time some of our 'kit' - a crane, a truck, a compressor, a dredger - exceeds 75 decibels, or 65 decibels if it's within a three feet of any nearby residence, we know it and respond immediately," I'm told. Indeed, before they ever began turning the first

spade of earth, Balfour Beatty and Costain environmental engineers made certain that the sub-contractors who supplied both companies with the enormous quantities of machinery they would require, above all had to be quiet. Some of it was re-designed to meet the specifications. Embankments were sprayed with a slurry of fast-growing and sound-absorbent grass seed. Hundreds of bales of hay were stacked around particularly noisy machinery to soak up the roar of exhausts.

What's it like to lose a world-wide family business? Sir Rocco Forte, son and heir of the hotel chain dynasty that spread to every continent under his father, Lord Forte, knows the feeling. Two years ago, the family lost a bitter and prolonged take-over battle from another British giant, the Granada Group, whose £3.9 billion bid won the day. So thorough was Granada's victory that today the Forte family cannot even use its own name on the new luxury hotels it is building in an attempt to gain a fresh foothold in the hostelry business.

One of the first steps the family took was a decision to accept a £4 million grant from the Cardiff Bay Development Corporation and other public agencies in Wales, enough to persuade Sir Rocco to invest the remainder of the £17 million required to build the Bay's striking St David's Hotel. Named after the patron saint of the Welsh who brought Christianity to the western edge of Great Britain, the 136 room facility is the first five-star hotel in Wales, a symbol both of the regeneration of Cardiff Bay and the Forte family.

Lancaster University scientists were even contracted to independently help formulate what the construction industry world-wide now regards as a model for the future in terms of community relations: to minimise disruption to the lives and routines of ordinary people who happen to find a mammoth engineering project on their doorstep.

To seal off the two rivers with a dam that will make up the lake required moving mind-boggling quantities of rock, steel, concrete and sand to and from the site. Complaints were few given the enormity of the task. In the first three years after Balfour Beatty and Costain were awarded the contract, there were fewer than 350. Typically perhaps, 80 per cent came from two households who regularly phoned the dedicated community relations helpline set up by the companies in the office of their community relations team.

To build a dam requires well-understood and commonly applied engineering technology that experts have known about for a century or more. But to build one within hearing distance of thousands of people, and to satisfy aesthetic demands as well, meant that for Balfour Beatty and Costain, this turned out to be a rather different, even pioneering project in engineering terms. The reason is that the Cardiff Bay

Barrage is more than a dam. It is central to the recreational objectives of the entire Bay endeavour. In some ways it is even artistic, this serpentine-shaped structure, topped by a walkway, cycle path and public park, which joins two shores. Why is it 'S' shaped? Because designers knew that a slinking wall of earth and concrete, topped with imaginative landscaping, would be more pleasing to the eye. When the 'button is pressed,' raising the huge sluice gates that will finally halt an eternity of ebbing and flooding tides, the people of Cardiff, of Wales and visitors from afar will find in the midst of this already appealing and engaging city, an attraction worthy of no small amount of marvel, meriting Raymond William's tribute to those of vision: "This is what men have built. Is not everything then possible?"

But look! Here come the crowds , pacing straight for the water, and

seemingly bound for a dive. Strange! Nothing will content them but

the extremist limit of the land.

Herman Melville

The dream of Lord Brooks and Lord Crickhowell is realised today as thousands can now 'see the sea' in Cardiff Bay,

lured by an almost primeval urge shared by all to be near the water. Herman Melville recognised it in *Moby Dick*.

Epilogue

"Americans abroad." The very phrase conjures up many images. As one London-based American journalist put it: "The British, for their part, think of Americans as a parade of plastic dolls, each with a prosthetic smile permanently bolted on and a tape-loop repeating 'Have a nice day!' where their brains ought to be." For many discerning Americans, the British, especially the English, while well-mannered, are distant, not exactly welcoming, and for the most part, devoid of any sense of emotion, much less the display of it. Whatever truth they may reveal, these are 'shoot from the hip' stereotypes, and we learn far more about one another from the more thoughtful and considered notions that have been recorded by visitors in both directions over the more than two centuries of the 'special relationship.'

For most of their history Americans have journeyed to Europe, with the earliest travellers finding a congenial complexity in European society that was wholly lacking in the simple world of America. The first who made what was an arduous and even perilous trip were not 'tourists.' I recall being on holiday in Brittany not long ago, and seeing a plaque on the quayside of a tiny French port noting the arrival in 1778 of Benjamin Franklin, an emissary of President Washington en route to Paris to negotiate still more help from the French in the revolt of the original thirteen American colonies against England. On his important diplomatic mission, Franklin had little time to devote to pondering local customs, architecture and manners.

All of that came much later when steam-driven ships, many of whose turbines spun from the intense heat produced by coal mined in South Wales, made travel to Europe for pleasure possible for a growing number of Americans, many driven by curiosity about the 'Old World.' As time went on, they included authors, artists and intellectuals who began the process - one that has become a veritable industry today - of endless comparisons of American and European life. But they also included a growing cadre of diplomats, ambassadors and consuls-general, posted to various European cities to represent the new republic, and almost all as a reward for political loyalty to one President or another. These men, for they were almost exclusively male, had the time and leisure that Benjamin Franklin never knew, and many of them used it to record their impressions. Hence, Dean Howells settled in Venice for four years as the American Consul, an unexpected dividend for having written President Lincoln's campaign biography. Howells spent much of his spare time penning *Venetian Life*, a charming portrait of that immortal Italian city that makes perceptive observations many modern writers overlook. Similarly, Nathaniel Hawthorne, already an established and popular American novelist, was appointed by his former classmate, President Franklin Pierce, as Consul to Liverpool, the British seaport that enjoyed a thriving trade with the United States. During his ten year stint in the United Kingdom, and later Italy, Hawthorne travelled widely in England and Scotland and recorded his observations in *Our Old Home*. It was badly received among the English literati, prompting

Hawthorne to scathingly remark that "The monstrosity of self-conceit is such that anything short of unlimited adoration impresses them as malicious caricature." There is no record of Hawthorne travelling across the Mersey to nearby Wales, and more's the pity since his thoughts on the other parts of the United Kingdom seem almost as fresh and perceptive today as they were when Americans first read them more than one hundred years ago. Search where you may, early and even contemporary American impressions of Wales are a scarce literary commodity. But there is one.

The criticism Hawthorne endured from the London press is not how the literary efforts of the American Consul for Wales, Wirt Sikes, were greeted when, in 1879, he produced a book with the rather bizarre title of *British Goblins*. Living in Cardiff, and very much a part of the city's growing intellectual, commercial and social life,

Sikes was - as far as I know - the first American to write about Wales. In its review of his book, the London Times wrote that "There is plenty of learning and critical knowledge displayed in his work as well as mere industry." What was Sikes about in *British Goblins*? Best to let him explain it: "In a certain sense, Wales may be spoken of as the cradle of fairy legend," he wrote in his very first lines. "It is not now disputed that from the Welsh were borrowed many of the first subjects of composition in the literature of all the cultivated peoples of Europe," he went on. Sikes had spent a great deal of time and effort accumulating stories from Welsh mythology, convinced as he was that "Among the vulgar in Wales, the belief in fairies is less nearly extinct than casual observers would be likely to suppose."

As fascinating as Sikes' thoughts are on the subject, I became much more interested in his second book,

Rambles and Studies in South Wales. Written as a series of articles for three of America's best-known magazines of the time, including the hugely popular Harper's, Sikes must have been the first American to tell his countrymen of Wales. At the time of his appointment he was unable to find, even in the cavernous and vast archives of the Congressional Library in Washington, anything on Wales. Now, having arrived in Cardiff, Sikes set out to put the Principality firmly at the forefront of American minds.

His views of the *'Sea, the Land, the City and the Bay,'* I commend in contrast to my own. Evidently not many of the Welsh have read it. I know that to be the case since the library copy I have has only been borrowed on two occasions in the past thirteen years. I saved reading *Rambles and Studies in South Wales* until this moment, not wanting Sike's views to impinge on my own. I need not have postponed the pleasure because it turns out that Consul Sikes and I are of one mind about Cardiff, the Welsh and their intriguing country. And many of the conclusions he reached more than a century ago seem as relevant today as they were for the readers of Harper's. Take, for example, his remark about the irrelevance of Wales in the minds of the English:

> South Wales is *terra incognita* to most Englishmen . . . to bury oneself in some remote village of South Wales appears to be a Londoner's strongest expression of complete isolation from the world.

Or, his puzzlement at the ordinary Welshman's knowledge of the richness of his country's literature, a characteristic that he felt left the English far behind:

> To hear a poor and grimy Welshman, who looks as if he might not have a thought above bread and beer, talk about the poets and poetry

of his native land, ancient and modern, is an experience which, when first encountered, gives the stranger quite a shock of agreeable surprise. Or, the peculiar contentment the Welsh get from simply 'staying put.' A conspicuous instance is the borough of Aberavon, in Glamorganshire, which has been termed the "community of the Joneses." The patriarchal owner of the valley of Cwm Avon lately said of it, in a letter to the London Times, "Few who came to Cwm Avon ever cared to leave it, and you will find families so intermixed that it is difficult to tell the remote and intricate degrees of relationship which exist." This modern Arcadia is not pastoral, as it happens; it is a mining community of some 8,000 souls, and exists within a mile and a half of a railway station,

an hour's drive from Cardiff, the Welsh metropolis; yet the population is known to have remained almost unchanged, except by the process of nature, for the past 200 years.

Sikes ranged far and wide in his comments, offering Americans probably their first introduction to Wales and Cardiff, a city he described as "clean and handsome, with broad streets and fine edifices, and a clear blue sky overhead." Sikes, appointed to his post by President Rutherford Hayes, was more than a perceptive observer of Wales and Welsh life, he was also a working diplomat, charged especially with the responsibility of ensuring that the growing trade between Wales and America continued to thrive, and thrive it did:

As regards its relations with American shipping, Cardiff is the second seaport town of Great Britain, the first being Liverpool. A greater number of American ships yearly arrive at and sail from Cardiff than from London.

He took great pride from the fact that "A striking feature of Cardiff's provision shops, which abound, is the presence of great quantities of canned eatables from America." But Sikes could not know any more than his Welsh hosts, that this bustling, hustling, booming European port was headed for hard times. He was there to see Victorian Cardiff flourish: the first buildings in the stunning civic centre of Cathays Park, the city's library where he was honoured to lay the foundation stone, the proposal for a university; all surely portents of a secure and unassailable future. At one point he remarks that "coal deposits are deemed well-nigh inexhaustible."

The Cardiff and Wales Wirt Sikes described to tens of thousands of American readers of Harper's, and my own observations are rather like two historical bookends: a lot happened in between. Two world wars, the dethroning of 'King Coal,' a grinding and economically punishing depression, and of course, the virtual disappearance of Cardiff docks. Were Sikes able to leap over the decades and see the Welsh 'metropolis' today, I have little doubt how he would react. "This," he would say, "is the rightful fulfilment of the city's destiny, and a tribute to the miraculous resilience and vision of its people."

My conclusion precisely.

Cardiff Bay

...enjoy